I0016761

SHOWME™ GUIDES
Managing an Online Business with
Open Source Commerce Programs

NOTICES

showme guides managing an online business with open source commerce programs

©2009 Kerry Watson
Pithy Productions, Inc.

Originally released as Managing an Online Business with osCommerce, for osCommerce, CRE Loaded, Zen Cart, Cube Cart, CartXpress, osC-MAX

All rights reserved. No part of this book shall be reproduced, stored in a retrieval system, or transmitted by any means, electronic, mechanical, photocopying, recording, or otherwise, without written permission from the publisher. No patent liability is assumed with respect to the use of the information contained herein. Although every precaution has been taken in the preparation of this book, the publisher and author assume no responsibility for errors or omissions. Neither is any liability assumed for damages resulting from the user of the information contained herein.

Printed in the USA
March, 2009

TRADEMARKS & INTELLECTUAL PROPERTY

All terms mentioned in this book that are known to be trademarks or service marks have been appropriately denoted to the best of our knowledge. Pithy Productions cannot attest to the accuracy of the information. Use of a term in this book should not be regarded as affecting the validity of any trademark or service mark. osCommerce is released under the GNU Public License. Pithy Productions is a trademark of Pithy Productions, Inc. CRE Loaded is a trademark of Chain Reaction Web. Cube Cart is a trademark of Devellion Limited. osC-MAX is a trademark of AA Box Web Hosting. Magento is a trademark of Irubin Consulting Inc.

WARNING AND DISCLAIMER

THE AUTHOR, PITHY PRODUCTIONS INC., AND THE SHOWME GUIDES BOOK SERIES ARE NOT OWNED BY OR AFFILIATED WITH OSCOMMERCE, CRE LOADED ECOMMERCE, ZEN CART, OSCMAX, AABOX, DEVELLION LTD., IRUBIN CONSULTING OR ANY OTHER PROGRAM MENTIONED IN THIS BOOK.

Every effort has been made to make this book as complete and accurate as possible, but no warranty or fitness is implied. The information is provided on an AS-IS basis. The author and the publisher have neither liability nor responsibility to any person or entity with respect to any loss or damages arising from the information contained in this book.

Table of Contents

Welcome to your new store!

Your store and version

How to log onto your "Employees Only" page for the first time

Your private user name and password

To change the wording on your Home Page

How to add a new product to your store

How to change a product description

How to change a product photo

How to edit other pages like Privacy, Shipping, etc.

How to add new pages to your store

How to change the email address where the 'Contact Us" customer enquiries are sent

Get copies of orders or customer enquiries automatically emailed to you and/or another person

Create shipping labels, invoices, packing slips, and update my new orders

How to change the names of product categories

Find out what products your visitors are looking at

A. Before you start your store

B. Under Construction

How much time to devote to each phase?

What happens during the Design phase?

What happens during the Programming phase?

What happens during the Testing phase?

What happens during Product Data Entry phase?

What happens during Acceptance phase?

What happens during Launch phase?

What do I do if things go wrong?

Reporting a problem to your techie

Finding other sources of tech help

C. Open for Business

What do I do first?

How do you know when you have customers?

Your first sale!

Getting return customers

When do you know you are out of start-up mode?

Who is in your store right now?

Who are your best customers?

Other reports

Monthly sales/tax report

Detailed Custom Reporting

Are search engines really important?

What do search engines want?

How do you get listed with the search engines?

Three big, dirty secrets about search engines

Ten Steps to Set Search Engine "Bait" and get your open

source commerce store listed with the major search engines

What about ad banners?

Don't forget traditional marketing!

Incorporate strategic customers' feedback

Introduction

About the ShowMe Guide Series

Every book in the **ShowMe™ Guide Series** is based on ACTUAL USAGE in an ecommerce store. We show you with actual screenshots, step-by-step what the program REALLY does -- not what their marketing department says it does, or what it *should* do. That's why we call it "ShowMe!"

The exclusive **ShowMe Guides** logo assures you that this book contains practical information that you can immediately put to use. Each topic has all the information you need, and no jargon. Just turn to the section you want and, voila! - you *know* that every instruction shows you exactly:

1. WHO has the right skill level to perform this task.
2. WHAT the task is.
3. WHY and WHEN you might want to do this - plenty of examples.
4. WHERE - LOTS of good screenshots show you exactly what to do.
5. HOW - Exact instructions showing what to change, and exactly what to change it to.

The **ShowMe Guides** quality seal guarantees that you *won't* find page after page of filler. We know you're busy, and if you wanted a general book on Internet History or PHP Programming, you'd be reading that book instead of ours.

About the author

 The author of the osCommerce Technical and User Manual Series, Kerry Watson joined the Open Source movement in 1996 as the Producer for the Netscape Navigator website. She holds an MBA and a Bachelor's Degree in Sociology and Communication. In 1999 she founded Pithy Productions, Inc., a web project management company that specializes in helping non-technical people with custom open source commerce websites.

Other helpful books in this series

These books will be especially useful to new and non-technical users:

ShowMe Guides User Manual Series
www.oscommercemanuals.com

Easy to understand user manuals for many open source commerce programs, including:

- osCommerce
- CRE Loaded
- Zen Cart
- osCMAX
- Magento
- PrestaShop

Icons used in this book:

I have used a number of special icons to make using this book easier. They are as follows:

 INFORMATION: Useful information related to the subject.

 TIME SAVING TIP: This is something important that will make your project much easier.

 CAUTION: Follow directions exactly, this is easy to mess up.

 TECHNICAL STUFF: Unless you love the technical stuff, this is something that a programmer or technical person should do for you.

 DANGER: Don't push the button unless you really, really, really know what you are doing!

Feedback, please!

I welcome your comments. Please feel free to email me to let me know what helped and what didn't, or what you'd like to see covered in future editions. Did you puzzle over something? Please tell me! Help others who may puzzle too, by sending me a note to me at talkback@oscommercemanuals.com.

Please note that I cannot personally help you with technical problems related to the topic of this book. Due to the high volume of mail I receive, I might not be able to reply personally to every message.

KERRY WATSON
www.osCommerceManuals.com

Jump Start Guide

My promise to you: NO TECHNICAL JARGON!

WELCOME TO YOUR NEW STORE!

Please ask your store builder what kind of store and version YOUR store is, for example, osCommerce #<u>MS2.2</u> :

My store and version # is:

osCommerce _____	osCMAX _____	CartXpress _____
CRE Loaded _____	Cube Cart _____	Zen Cart _____
Magento _____		

The instructions for all 7 of these programs are nearly identical. Sometimes a button has a different name, or the instructions are slightly different, so watch for the name of your store for special instructions, *like this:*

Zen Cart: click the E  Button to edit.

How to log onto your "Employees Only" page for the first time:

Every online store has an "Employees Only" door that requires a username and password as the key. Behind this door you will check on orders, mark orders as shipped, and even change the way your store looks. You will administer your store simply by changing the answers on various forms.

OPEN Internet Explorer and type your *real store name, with "admin" after it,* like this:

 TIP: Add this to your "FAVORITES" List NOW! You will be unlocking this door every day.

Log In

Type your email address and the password given to you by the builder of your store. Contact your store builder if you do not have one.

Please record your email address and password here.

TIP: If you lose or forget your password, click "Password forgotten" and enter your email address. If your builder set up an admin account in your name, your store will automatically email a new password to you! If this does not work, tell your store builder.

TIP: If the username your techie gives you is admin@localhost.com and your password is admin, then stop! Ask your Techie to delete it and create a unique username and password for you.

This brings you to your **private MAIN Administration Page:**

Note: The look of your private main Administration page may vary, but the main groups will be the same.

Zen Cart: The groupings are across the top instead of in the page.

Magento: The groupings are across the top instead of in the page.

Cube Cart: The groupings are in the left column.

 BIG TIP: Always change ONE thing, then immediately LOOK AT IT IN YOUR STORE (Open another browser window with CTRL-N).

1. To change the wording on your Home Page text:

Changing the Home Page text is done slightly differently for each of the open source commerce programs, but the Home Page text you are changing is the text in the center of your home or main website page:

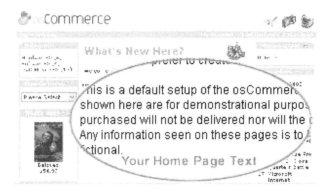

osCommerce MS2.2, CartXpress: Type the changes you want in an email or in Microsoft Word, and send them to your store builder. He or she must make the changes by programming them for you. OR ask your techie to install an add-on contribution to make editing easy for you, such as a program called "TinyMCE." If you have TinyMCE installed, follow the CRE Loaded instructions below.

CRE Loaded: On your main Admin menu, under **Content Manager,** click **DEFINE MAINPAGE**. (See illustration on next page)

Simply change the text to what you want. When you finish, click the **SAVE button.**

Magento: On your main Admin menu, under **CMS** (Content Management System), click **MANAGE PAGES** and select the **HOME** page from the "Identifier" column. Type your text in the "Content" form box and click the SAVE PAGE Button.

Cube Cart: Click Documents Homepage. Type the text you wish, then click the UPDATE HOMEPAGE button.

osC-MAX: Click Catalog, then click DEFINE MAINPAGE. Type the text you wish, then click the UPDATE button.

Zen Cart: Click TOOLS, then click Define Pages Editor. Then in the box that says "TEXT EDITOR" click HTMLarea, and in the box "Select a file to edit." click the page define_main_page.php Type the text you wish. When you finish, click the SAVE button.

2. How to add a new product to your store:

From your private main administration page, go to Catalog - Category/Products. Click the icon that looks like a file folder until you are in the category (department) where you wish to put your new product.

 Magento: Catalog - Manage Products, then click the ADD PRODUCT Button.

Click the NEW PRODUCT Button. Fill in at least the product NAME, MODEL, and WEIGHT. You can always change product details later! When you finish, click the PREVIEW button, then click the SAVE button.

TIP: If you are a slow typist OR if you get interrupted while you are editing your product, like an automatic timed lock, your store may shut you out for security. If this happens, YOU WILL LOSE ALL YOUR EDITS.

To avoid losing your edits, 1) draft your text in a program like Microsoft Word or WordPerfect, or 2) type them in an email and save it, or 3) hit the SAVE button at least every 15 minutes, then return to your typing.

3. How to change a product description:

Go to Catalog - Category/Products. Your store builder has probably arranged your products into categories, like the departments in a store. Each category is represented by a File Folder icon. Click the Folders until you are in the right category.

Magento: Catalog - Manage Products, then click the name of the product you want to edit.

Highlight the product you wish to edit by clicking the product name, then click the EDIT [edit] Button.

Zen Cart: Highlight the product you wish to edit by clicking the product name, then click the E ⓔ Button.

Edit the product description as you wish.

When you finish, click the PREVIEW [preview] button waaaay down at the bottom right of the screen (you may have to scroll to find it) then click the UPDATE [update] button.

4. How to change a product photo:

What we're doing here: first you will open the product that needs a new picture, then browse your computer to find the picture. The program uploads it for you when you click the Save button. (**CRE Loaded** can upload many extra product photos, see separate directions below).

On your private main administration page, again go to Catalog - Category/ Products. Click the File Folders icon until you find the product you want to add a photo to.

Magento: Catalog - Manage Products and click the product, then in left column click IMAGES.

Click the EDIT Button.

Zen Cart: the E ⓔ Button.

To change the product photo, click the BROWSE or BROWSE FILES Button and find the photo on your computer: `Browse...`

Cube Cart: click UPLOAD NEW IMAGE Button, then click BROWSE Button

... but you're not quite done yet! You MUST click the PREVIEW button. `preview`

Magento: UPLOAD FILES Button, then click Thumbnail, Small Image, and Base Image radio buttons, then click the SAVE Button.

Cube Cart: UPLOAD, Close Window

And then click the UPDATE button: `update`

Cube Cart: EDIT Button.

...NOW your new product image will appear with this product.

Additional Images in CRE Loaded:

On your private main administration page, go to Catalog - Category/Products. Click the File Folders icon until you find the product you wish to add a photo to.

Click the EDIT Button and then:

1. On the PRODUCTS page Scroll down to the Products Image box, then click the PICTURE Icon.

Products Image:
Main Image used in
catalog & description pages.

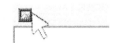

The "PICTURE" Icon (arrow)

TIP: If you do not see the PICTURE icon shown above, your builder will need to upload pictures for you OR you need to switch to Internet Explorer when adding pictures.

2. and then click the BROWSE button to find the product picture on your computer. When you find the image you want, click the OPEN button...

3. And then click the UPLOAD button.

You MUST click the PREVIEW button. `preview`

And then click the UPDATE button: `update`

NOW your new product image will appear with this product.

TIP: Always LOOK in your store at the changes you make. Open ANOTHER browser window by clicking START - Internet Explorer, and type the address of your store to LOOK at the new image!

TIP: If you don't see the new image, click the REFRESH button in Internet Explorer.

4. How to edit other pages like Privacy, Shipping, etc.

Information
Shipping and returns
Privacy
Gift Voucher FAQ
Links
Contact Us

 osCommerce MS2.2, CartXpress: Type the changes you want in an email or in Microsoft Word, and send them to your store builder. He or she must make the changes by programming them for you. OR ask your techie to install an add-on contribution to make editing easy for you, such as a program called "TinyMCE." If you have TinyMCE installed, follow the CRE Loaded instructions below.

CRE Loaded: Click Info System - Info Manager. Click the name of the file you wish to change, and click the ✐ Edit icon.

Magento: Click CMS - Manage Pages. Click the name of the file you wish to change, and it loads on your screen. Type the text you wish. When you finish, click the SAVE Button.

osC-MAX: Click Catalog - then click the name of the page: Privacy Page, Conditions Page, or Shipping Page. Type the text you wish. When you finish, click the SAVE button.

Cube Cart: Click Documents - Site Documents, then click the "Edit" link next to the name of the page: About us, Contact Us, Privacy Policy or Terms & Conditions. Type the text you wish. When you finish, click the UPDATE DOCUMENT button.

Zen Cart: Click TOOLS, then click Define Pages Editor. In the box that says "TEXT EDITOR" click HTMLarea, and in the box "Select a file to edit." click the page define_privacy.php Type the text you wish. When you finish, click the SAVE button.

5. How to add new pages to your store:

 osCommerce MS2.2, osC-MAX, CartXpress: Type the changes you want in an email or in Microsoft Word, and send them to your store builder. He or she must make the changes by programming them for you. OR ask your techie to install an add-on contribution to make editing easy for you, such as a program called "TinyMCE." If you have TinyMCE installed, follow the CRE Loaded instructions below.

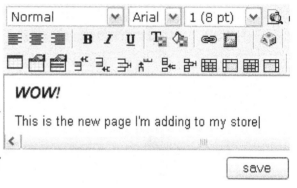

CRE Loaded:

Click CONTENT MANAGER - Info Manager. Click the NEW button, in the box named TITLE type a title, and in the box named DESCRIPTION type the contents of the new page.

When you finish, click the INSERT Button, then click the GREEN Button so customers can see the new page.

Magento: Click CMS - Manage Pages, then in the top right corner click the ADD PAGE Button. Give the page a title, a file name with no spaces such as about-us or our-specials-today, change status to ENABLED and type the text you wish in the CONTENT box. When you finish, click the SAVE Button.

Cube Cart: Click Documents - Site Documents, then in the top right corner click the "Add New" link. Type the text you wish. When you finish, click the SAVE button.

Zen Cart: Click TOOLS, then click Define Pages Editor. Then in the box that says "TEXT EDITOR" click HTMLarea, and in the box "Select a file to edit." click the page define_ page_2.php Type the text you wish. When you finish, click the SAVE button. Now to make this page visible to your customers, click CONFIGURATION - Define Page Status, click the name "Define Page 2" and then change the zero (OFF) to a "1" (ON).

6. How to change the email address where the 'Contact Us" customer enquiries are sent.

This is useful if you go on vacation and need someone else to tend your store.

Click CONFIGURATION - MY STORE

CubeCart: Configuration - General Settings
Zen Cart: Configuration - Email Options
Magento: System - Configuration - GENERAL - Contacts, Send Emails To.

... click "Email Address" then click the Edit button. When you finish click the Update button.

Magento: SAVE CONFIG Button.

My Store

Store Name
Store Owner
Store Logo
E-Mail Address

7. Get copies of orders or customer enquiries automatically emailed to you and/or another person.

Configuration - My Store - click "**Send Extra Order Emails To**" then click the Edit button.

My Store

Title

E-Mail From

Country

Zone

Expected Sort Order

Expected Sort Field

Switch To Default Language Currency

Send Extra Order Emails To

Magento: System - Configuration - SALES - Sales Emails, then Send Order Email Copy To

Zen Cart: Click Configuration – Email Options – Send Copy of Admin Orders Status Emails To.

When you finish, click the UPDATE **button.**

Magento: SAVE CONFIG Button.

If more than one person needs to receive copies of orders, put a comma after each email address like this:

name@address1.com, name@address2.com

8. Create shipping labels, invoices, packing slips, and update my new orders

1. On your private main administration page, click CUSTOMERS/ ORDERS - ORDERS.

Magento: SALES - ORDERS.

The newest orders will display first.

Orders

		Order ID:	
		Status:	All Orders

Customer	Order Total purchased	Date	Status	Action	[6525] 12/18/2005 13:50:57
Joe Finkelstein	$45.00	12/13/05	Pending	ⓘ	edit
Sally Mustang	$37.45	12/13/05	Pending	ⓘ	delete
Dawg Hershey	$21.00	12/12/05	Pending	ⓘ	update
Joel Harris	$15.95	12/12/05	Pending	ⓘ	invoice
					packing slip

To process the order, click a customer's name, then click the EDIT button.

Cube Cart: click the customer's **Order Number**.

Orders

Customer:	Jane Imalotta 123 45th St. San City, TX 78234	Shipping Address:	Jane Imalotta PO Box 74 San City, TX 78234	Billing Address:	Jane Imalotta 123 45th St. San City, TX 78234
Telephone Number:	777-777-7777				
E-Mail Address:	aa@aa.com				
IP Address:	70.66.29.125				

Invoice No. 1231

Date Purchased: 12/13/05 7:56:00 PM

Payment Method: Credit Card 1234 5678 9123 4567 Exp. 12/09

Highlight the shipping address and copy it for

an address label with EDIT - COPY.

2. PRINT A SHIPPING LABEL. Copy the shipping address by highlighting the shipping address, then in Internet Explorer select EDIT - COPY.

Open Microsoft Word, Stamps.com, or the postage program you wish to use with your shipping labels) and

Paste the shipping address into your shipping label by clicking where you want it and in Word, select EDIT - PASTE.

3. PRINT A PACKING SLIP. Click the PACKING SLIP button, then in Internet Explorer click FILE - PRINT.

4. MARK THIS ORDER STATUS COMPLETED AND EMAIL COMMENTS TO CUSTOMER. Click the "Notify Customer" box next to STATUS (see picture below) and select Delivered. Add any comments you wish such as "Thank you for your order! We have shipped it via." then click the UPDATE Button.

IMPORTANT: IF YOU DO NOT WANT THE COMMENTS IN THE COMMENTS BOX EMAILED TO THE CUSTOMER, YOU MUST UN-CHECK THE "Notify Customer" box:

Comments

```
Any comments you type here will be SENT TO THE CUSTOMER
(unless you UN-CHECK the "Notify Customer" box below) AND
saved in the store record that the customer can see when
they log on. |
```

Status: Delivered [3] ⌄   update

Notify Customer: ☑   **Append Comments:** ☑

How to change the names of product categories

Let's say you wish to change the category name in the box on the right box from "Caps" to "Hats."

On your private main administration page, go to Catalog - Category/Products. Each link is represented by a 📁 File Folder. Click the Folders until you find the one you wish to change.

Categories

Action Figures (2)
Bracelets (1)
Bumper Stickers (9)
Buttons (1)
Caps (2)
CDs/DVDs (8)
Clearance
**Holiday
Specials!** (4)
Mugs
Posters (5)
T-Shirts (20)

Magento: CATALOG - MANAGE CATEGORIES, then in the left column click the category you wish to edit, type the new name in the NAME box and click the SAVE CATEGORY Button.

When you see the folder you want, click the category NAME, not the folder picture. This highlights the folder.

**This will edit the above link
named
"Cool Free Stuff"**

NOW click the EDIT Button

Zen Cart: the E Button

... then edit as you wish.

 TIP: If you don't see the name of the folder you want any more, just click your browser's BACK button until you do.

Find out what products your visitors are looking at:

What products are visitors looking at, and how many times have they viewed them?

Best Viewed Products

No.	Products	Viewed
01.	CRE LOADED 6.1 Users Manual (English)	5301
02.	osCommerce Users Manual V2. (English)	3305

On your private main administration page, click REPORTS - PRODUCTS VIEWED

Cube Cart: Statistics, View Stats.
Magento: REPORTS - PRODUCTS - Most Viewed.

Find out what products your visitors are actually purchasing:

What products are visitors actually purchasing, and how many have you sold?

Best Products Purchased

No.	Products	Purchased
01.	Ten Sneaky Tips & Tricks for osCommerce	819
02.	TOP 7 FREE or CHEAP Power Tools for osCommerce	639
03.	TOP 10 Mistakes osCommerce Developers Make	587

On your private main administration page, click REPORTS - PRODUCTS PURCHASED:

Magento: REPORTS - PRODUCTS - Bestsellers.

Find out who your best customers are:

Who is purchasing the most products from you?

Best Customer
Orders-Total

01. Marilyn Kagda $69.50
02. Kerry Boston $39.95
03. Ben Peterson $45.90

On your private main administration page, click REPORTS -ORDERS TOTAL:

Magento: REPORTS - CUSTOMERS - Customers by orders total.

Send an email or newsletter to all or just one of your customers:

On your private main administration page, select TOOLS - SEND EMAIL.

Magento: NEWSLETTER - Newsletter Templates - Add New Template.

As show below select the recipient's name, and then type a message just like a regular email:

Send Email To Customers

Customer: | To All Newsletter Subscribers | ▼
Select Customer
All Customers
To All Newsletter Subscribers

From:

Subject:

Message:

send mail

Magento: Click SAVE TEMPLATE Button, then from the top bar navigation click NEWSLETTER - Newsletter Queue. Click your newsletter, then in the QUEUE DATE START box enter the date and time you want the newsletter to be sent. Click the SAVE NEWSLETTER Button.

What else can I do with my open source commerce store?

Well, there is a lot more you can do with it, but this covers the main things you need to do to get your store jump-started. If you wish to become an advanced user, including a few *optional* technical things, get our user manual for your program.

1

Managing an online business with open source commerce

Now anyone can run an online store that would have cost a million dollars a few years ago. You don't have to be technical or have special knowledge to do it.

When he first invented the telephone, Alexander Graham Bell is often quoted to have prophesized, "It is my firm belief that the day will come when there will be a telephone in every town in America."

No long ago I realized that some day many ordinary, non-technical people would have their own website. Then my customers began dreaming up ideas for their second, third, and fourth websites, and these websites are usually an ecommerce site that needs open source commerce.

Who is This Book For?

This book is for anyone who has an idea for something they wish to sell on the Internet, whether products or services. It is written without technical jargon for NON-technical people – store owners, managers, or administrators – who wish to operate a full or part-time online business selling goods (or possibly services) over the Internet.

You may work in a large corporation that wants a highly customized open source commerce site, or you may work alone from your dining table at home. Many other open source commerce store owners have a "day job" and operate their store in their spare time. You bought this book because you are ready to do it now, and you want to make sure an open source commerce store is the right program to do that for you. That's fine: this book will be JUST RIGHT for you.

Every open source commerce store owner should have a technical person to call on for help, whether that's a friend, your webmaster, or your web host or Internet Service Provider (ISP). *Everyone – even the most technical person - needs someone who knows more than they do.*

Don't worry if you don't know who your technical person is yet; we will help you identify the best for your needs later in the book.

Once you are finished with this book, if you want to get into more advanced stuff, then one of my User Manuals will be right for you. It includes many things that you can do using the Administrative Module in your browser. It is available from Amazon.com or from my website, **www.oscommercemanuals.com**.

What does this book cover?

This book covers everything you need to know about planning, organizing, managing, quantifying, and improving an online store using the most popular open source commerce programs.

What kind of experience do I need?

You are not expected to have any specialized experience to manage an open source commerce store, only the ability to use a web browser like Internet Explorer and a little business sense.

How to use this book:

This book is made so you can easily skim the headings and pick just the topics that you are interested in. However, you will get a much better view of open source commerce store management if you read through the entire book once. Then go back and use this book as a reference any time you need it.

2

A day in the life of a real online store

This can be your dream job, if you make it. It can also be your worst nightmare if you let your store take charge of you! Come and take a look at a typical day in the life of a full-time online store owner:

You wake up with the sun, no alarm clock anymore. Coffee and newspaper, you're eager to see what happened in your store overnight but understand that you must try to keep normal work hours. It's too easy to work all the time and burn yourself out. You got into this to enjoy yourself, remember?

Opening Time

It's 9 am and time to "open your store." You click your browser and immediately see that your store is fine—you have set your browser "start" page to your store so you can easily keep tabs on it. You put on a fresh pot of coffee while you download your emails with copies of orders that came in overnight as well as enquiries from people around the world and from night owls in your country.

Checking new messages

You have a mailbox full of new messages, since your store is open around the clock the citizens of Asia and Europe browsed your store and bought your goods as you slept. The U.S. is just waking up with you so you have few sales from them yet.

You receive a copy of each sales receipt as it is sent to your customers, and the matching credit card sales receipt. You also receive pre-sales inquiries. Most critical are the emails sent to your "Customer Service" email address, because those are support issues by frustrated customers. Luckily your emails are filtered into folders so you can quickly prioritize and identify the emergencies.

Taking care of customers

You have learned to think of your store like a restaurant: people who enter are hungry for your goods, and easily upset until they are full. You quickly scan the pleas for help and politely set the ones who need support onto the right path to get it.

Hmmm, you note that two people have recently had trouble with the same page, so you make a note to yourself: Self, it's time to re-write that page. If one person complains that they didn't understand it, maybe they just had a bad day. If two report it, it's time to pay attention.

Surf to your bank

Now, with coffee in hand, the fun part: check your bank balance online since yesterday. Wow! It was a good day. It could have just as easily been an off-day too, though; the orders seem to ebb and flow. Customers all seem to order at the same time on the same gloomy days, and few orders come in on those first gorgeous spring days. Each store and even each product can have a different "busiest" day of the week.

See who's in your store, right now

You can't resist taking a look at how many customers are in your store right now. So you click Who's Online: 6 customers are meandering around in your store, right now! One has put something in their shopping cart, good. One is looking at your information pages. One is looking at your most popular product, and the other 3 just got there, with their referral ID from a sister site still showing. Another just registered for a new account! This makes your store feel alive, and you're refreshed.

Pick up and process your new sales orders!

Time to fulfill orders before the postman arrives, so you click Orders and view the list of most recent orders. You've priced all your goods so you can tell by the total sale price exactly what goods the customer ordered without clicking each sale. For example, odd prices are download goods, even prices are items you need to ship on the next business day. There's no reason to open up all the download orders since you already matched them up to sales receipts and you know they went through just fine.

You quickly copy and paste the shipping address for each order into a Word document that's set up for labels, also noting on each shipping label the Order Number, Date, and Product Model Number.

You also open a text document you call "Snippets" which contains the text of the various things you say to customers over and over, said in the best and most polite way.

You open your Stamps.com program (or UPS.com, FedEx, etc.) and log on for online postage and labels that will be printed on your printer and slapped onto each package.

After you copy each customer's address and paste it into the online postage program, you paste into your store's "comments" box the appropriate comments thanking them for the order. Your comment also tells the customer that their order is being processed, and will be shipped out the next business day. You change their order status to "PROCESSING" print a packing slip, click "UPDATE" and move on to the next order. You repeat this several times, going back to check a day or two in the past to be sure you didn't miss any recent orders.

Now you have a stack of packing slips and shipping address labels to pull off your printer, and you take them over to your shipping center.

Package up your orders

In your shipping center, which is really just a big closet you have set up for shipping, you have envelopes in two different sizes for single and multiple purchases. You count up the single orders and multiple orders, and pull the appropriate envelopes and merchandise to fit. You are a shipping machine as you affix the label, drop in the merchandise, insert the appropriate packing slip, and seal the flap.

You still need to affix the customs receipt to the international orders, slap the second shipping label on that, and stamp the package with "Priority Mail" "Air Mail" or other appropriate shipping rate.

Last, you tape the flap and the shipping label with clear tape – you have learned that this avoids delays, returns and complaints – and at last you have packaged up the first order. You move onto the next order, and the next. Finally you have a neat stack which the postman picks up. Perfect timing!

Lunchtime

It's lunchtime, and you've learned to stand back from the computer and not touch the keyboard for at least one hour or you will quickly burn out. Okay, so your secret is that you have to set a timer to stay away from the keyboard. Go for a walk or run with the dog, exercise, read a book. Beeeep! You can come back to work now. It was never this fun working for someone else.

Check stock levels

Whether or not you use the store's inventory level checking, you visually check your stock levels and place re-orders when they reach a pre-set minimum level. Quick re-order emails to your suppliers telling them which credit card on file to use, and you are caught up.

Order office supplies

Next you place an online order for labels, boxes, and other accouterments of an online store. Mundane chores that must be done. Just like your product's stock levels, you know how long the typical lead time takes to get the supplies delivered to you.

Change order statuses to "shipped"

You still have that stack of delivery tracking receipts, and need to tell folks that their packages have shipped and give them their package tracking number so they can track the progress online without asking you for assistance. So in your online store you pull up Orders again, click the drop-down box to select all orders that have the status of "Processing" and click down the list pasting in their tracking numbers. You change the statuses to "Shipped" and you are done. The days that you are sure that you have not missed the postman, you can actually skip this step and optimistically change the status to Shipped as you are picking up and processing orders.

Proactive maintenance

Now it's time to fix those problems that at least two people have had with your store. Perhaps the language you used is not clear, the word uncommon, perhaps it's in a part of the page that the visitor's eye just naturally skips over. You take a look and make some adjustments, then repeat it on another page for extra luck. That should eliminate any customer complaints, on that issue anyway. You should be working on a newsletter to send out to those customers who subscribed, but you'll save that for tomorrow and work on it in your head until then.

Run some reports

Since you're already in your store's Admin, you need to check some reports. You look at Products Viewed Report to see what products are being looked at the most, then Products Purchased to compare the two. You need to file a sales tax report tomorrow with the state, but you have the Monthly Sales/Tax contribution installed, so you simply click that link and then click the "Save as CSV" button to save it as a spreadsheet to your computer. You open it in Excel, sort and play with it a bit, then print it out and save. Fun!

Add a new product

You have a new product coming out next Tuesday, so you need to start working on the product description about it. You open Products/Categories and add the new product. It takes longer than you expect, dreaming about what to say, and suddenly an hour has gone by.

Get a little bit ahead

If you're like many online store owners, you may also be the craftsman who makes the merchandise you sell. So now that it's late afternoon, it's time to get to your "real" work! You spend the rest of the day on your craft, and answering the occasional support emails that come in from your US customers (your international customers are now sleeping). Every now and then you see an order come in – ka-CHING! – but you know enough to leave them alone until you do them all in a batch the next morning or you'll find yourself working around the clock. This is your dream job! And you are in control.

3

Why open source commerce is so cool for you

Like so many people, you have a great idea for an online business.

The problem is, how do you get it on the Internet?

Open source commerce programs are designed for people like you. Normal, non-technical people who have a dream about an online business and wish to make it come true. Whether you want to sell a product, service, or a combination.

Why "open source commerce?" Why not some other ecommerce program or shopping cart?

open source commerce programs are not just "shopping carts" that lets customers choose more than one item and pay for it with a credit card. Oh yes, it allows you to accept payments online from checks and credit cards; accept payments from other countries and in other currencies; and even accept payments while you are in another country.

But open source commerce programs have become so much more. They have become "**store management programs.**" In the evolution of commerce, we went from counting on fingers to the abacus to the adding machine, to the cash register, to the physical store management program that tells the cashier that there is one more item in stock, for example.

Now open source commerce takes the online store one step further. It has a way to do *almost anything that you might want an online store to do*. Most users use it for a year or two before they realize all the things their store could be doing for them. That's great! Most other "shopping cart programs are like old-fashioned cash registers. You will outgrow them very quickly, and they cannot fulfill your needs so easily with built-in programs the way open source commerce can.

What *is* open source commerce?

In a nutshell, open source commerce programs are very popular, *FREE*, publicly-licensed, Amazon-style online ecommerce and online store management programs. They are powerful because they can easily be modified, customized, and have many add-on programs (called "contributions" because they are contributed for free) easily installed by programmers.

What kinds of things can open source commerce help me do?

- User-friendly, NON-technical management for NON-technical store owners using only your web browser (like Internet Explorer or Netscape)
- Have customer credit card payments automatically deposited in your bank account

- Lets customers choose what shipper to use, i.e. FedEx, USPS and have shipping cost automatically added to customer's total
- Add, Edit, and Remove products, product descriptions, product categories, manufacturers, customers, and product reviews
- Send emails or newsletters to one or all of your customers
- See which of your products are earning you the most money, which products people look at most, and which customers are best buyers
- Collect correct taxes on taxable goods
- Accept International Currencies and display your site in the language of your visitors' choice
- See how many folks are in your store at any given time, what page they are on, and what they are buying

Where did open source commerce come from?

The first open source commerce program, osCommerce, began as the idea of a man in Germany named Harald Ponce de Leon, and became a group project of a team of volunteers. Rather than hold tightly to the idea and limit its distribution, Harald decided to let anyone use or modify his program by releasing it under a program called the GNU Public License. Under this program, anyone can use the program for free, and even if you make an improvement to the program you can market it, but you also agree to donate a copy of the improvement back to the original project.

Today in addition to the original osCommerce, there are other programs that are built on and improve osCommerce, some that look and act like osCommerce but are not, and some that are inspired by osCommerce but programmed completely differently on the inside.

Contribution? What is a "contribution"?

An add-on improvement to the original program is called a "Contribution" since it is contributed back to the community. In this book I generally call them "add-on contributions" to make it clear that they are add-ons.

The different open source commerce programs

This GNU Public License has allowed the open source commerce community to flourish.

In the lifespan of a program like the original osCommerce, different programmers may have different philosophies about what is or is not important. The GNU public license allows these programmers to leave the original project and create a program of their own. If it uses the original program's code, then of course it must be contributed back (if they start from scratch, of course they do not). These similar programs are called "branches" or "offshoots" of the original, like a tree or a path on the ground.

This group includes:

Program name	Web pages (NOT websites) listed by Google
osCommerce MS2.2 – The original, stable, no added contributions, for minimalists who prefer full control.	**10,400,000 "Powered by osCommerce "and copyright** *Many of the below stores ALSO say "Powered by osCommerce" so this number may be over-counted.*

Zen Cart – optimized for ease of upgrading, changing templates, and definition of product features (size, color, etc.) A moderate number of contributions pre-installed and tested.	**502,000 with "Zen Ventures, LLC"**
CRE Loaded – optimized for the needs of small to large businesses and large numbers of products. Has the most useful add-on contributions pre-installed and tested.	**254,000 with "Supercharged by CRE Loaded"**
Cube Cart – Optimized for ease of installation by designers, with validated XHTML & CSS Code. A moderate number of contributions pre-installed and tested.	**703,000 with "Powered by CubeCart" and "Devellion." May be under-counted since users can pay a fee to remove the copyright statement.**
Magento - The newest open source commerce program, with whiz-bang features to knock out your customers and help them find the products they want. Programmed differently than the others, optimized for advanced designers and programmers, easy upgrades. A moderate number of add-ons with many more planned.	**239,000 with "Copyright Irubin."**
osC-MAX – optimized for the needs of larger retail operations and large numbers of products. Many contributions pre-installed and tested.	**545,000 with "Powered by osC-MAX"**
CartXpress – Optimized for small stores. A small number of contributions pre-installed and tested.	**Cannot determine since they do not include their own copyright statement in their program, only osCommerce.**

How do you choose the right version of open source commerce for you?

Well, each of the above versions has many satisfied users, and as you saw in the Jump Start chapter using the Admin is startlingly similar in all, so you know they are all good. I think the version you use should depend upon what your technical support person likes best. As I will repeat many times in this book, I recommend that everyone, no matter how technical or non-technical you are, should have a support person to rely on.

4

Do I have to do any technical stuff?

This is the nitty-gritty background information.

Your choice: Turnkey to Do-It-All-Yourself.

No, you don't have to do technical stuff, unless you wish to. Your options range among the following:

- **Turnkey *Custom* Store.** Purchase a complete, unique store done to your own exact custom specifications, tested, pre-loaded with your products and ready to sell. You just pay, have it 100% built to your specifications, "turn the key" and it's all yours.
- **Turnkey "*Spec*" or "Store-in-a-Box."** Purchase a complete, 100% finished store done "On Spec" pre-designed, tested, and pre-loaded with products ready to sell. For sale on Ebay and similar marketplaces. You just select the store you want, pay, "turn the key" and it's all yours.
- **Template Store.** Find a pre-designed template from a template shop and have them install the software and template for you. Template shops pool the creativity of designers and sell the same template a limited number of times, often 5 or 6 times, then retire the design. You may also pay 5-6 times the cost for a first-time exclusive template. You load your own products or pay someone to do it for you.

- **Template and a Freelance Programmer.** You pick the template you want, and hire a freelance programmer or agency to integrate it into the website you want. You may load your own products or pay someone to do it for you.

- **Template and Your Do-It-Yourself Skills.** After choosing the template you want, you attempt to integrate it into the shop that you or your web host have installed. Unfortunately templates are often put together in strange and inefficient ways, so this is not highly recommended.

- **No Template, no Freelancers, Your Do It Yourself Skills.** You may choose a program that already has several templates pre-installed, and you simply modify the one that is closest to your vision. If you have some design and html skills and like a technical challenge, this may appeal to you.

Why do I need a technical person?

Although you may have thoughts of one day becoming a "webmaster," it is actually a very rare individual who can create and maintain everything about a website on their own. I call it the "webmaster myth." Even the most advanced programmer has a programmer he or she can call on when they get stuck. **Most websites are a collaborative project of a *group* of people, each with very different talents**.

The *people* who contribute to a website:

- **A graphics artist** with web design experience will design a site with many programming tricks to make the site look very rich while loading quickly and efficiently. Once you have approved the final design, they will "slice" it and give the pieces to the programmer like a jigsaw puzzle to use during programming.
- **A programmer** or engineer-type person who thinks logically who programs the site to make it actually function as designed by the graphics artist.
- **A project manager** who keeps the project and people running smoothly and efficiently. They will get the cost estimate based on the artist's design and keep the project within your approved budget.
- **An account manager** is your advocate on the team so that when your desires conflict with what is most efficient for your website or your customers, a harmonious solution prevails.

The *things* that make up a website:

In addition to the many people who contribute to a website, every website has a bunch of different physical parts. They are:

1. **A Domain Name.** The address you type into the Location bar that usually starts with <u>www.</u>

2. **A Domain Name Registrar**. This is the company that buys the domain for you in your name, and reminds you each year to renew it or automatically renews it for you.

3. **A "Web Host."** A web host is a company that owns computers linked to the Internet where people like you can safely store their website files. These computers on which your website files are called "Web servers" because they "serve" the pages to you or your customers when you request them by typing the <u>www.</u> domain name in your browser. The web server is very similar to your personal computer, except it has specialized web server software on it to make it run efficiently. The web host company hires technical support people, makes back-up copies of your website in case the web server crashes, and should house the web servers in a fireproof, disaster-proof room.

4. **A Web Developer.** This is the general term for the people who build your website for you. They may just build it and leave you on your own after that, or you may decide to use them for ongoing web maintenance. The web developer may be an advertising or marketing agency, a specialized web development or web design company, an individual, or even you if you are technically inclined.

5. **Optional: An osCommerce Web Template Company.** The look and feel of an osCommerce website can look pretty plain, but templates can jazz them up so much that you don't recognize them. Your template company is the best installer, even if you use a web developer to do the rest of your website.

6. **A Web Maintenance Company.** This is the person or company who maintains your website for you – makes periodic changes to the text or layout, adds or enables contributions if you wish to upgrade something, adds email boxes if you need them, checks with the web host or developer if it seems that your website is "not working" to find out what's wrong, and in

general acts as the intermediary for the many people and services involved in keeping your website going.

Pulling together all the people and things:

Such a dizzying array of people, computers, and services involved in a single website! How do you keep it all straight? How do you know what to do first, whom to hire, how to organize it?

Simplicity is the answer. You can involve a half-dozen or more people or companies, but the fewer you use, the simpler your life will be. Let's say your website stops working. If you use many different companies, each company will need to check to see if something they did is the cause of the problem. If not, all they can do is rule themselves out and recommend that you contact the NEXT company on your list; they cannot test the other company's pieces. However, if you've consolidated your web services, you may have only one person or company to call on.

 TIP: Life is easy and happy if you consolidate all your web services so you have ONE PERSON TO CALL in case of problems.

 TIP: The more people who work on your site, the higher your frustration levels will be. You may like to shop for the lowest price of each element. This is super until your first problem or outage, then you will pay it all back and more.

Getting your website:

1. **Decide on a Domain Name**. Start by finding a good, unique domain name. Type the names you like in your browser to see if it can be found. If it's not found, the chances are pretty good that it is available. The best domain names will contain words that people use to search for you on Google or other search engines.
2. **Find some sites or templates that you like**. This will help you describe what you want to your technical pro.
3. *Let your technical pro take over from here.* They will advise you on which names are good for search engines, which designs or templates will work best for you, which version of osCommerce they recommend. You aren't expected to know everything yourself.

5

Deciding on an online business

Some products work better than others with online sales. Make sure your store is one of the successful ones by selecting the right online business.

Finding the right online business idea

Will YOUR store be successful? What kind of online business is most likely to succeed? How do you decide what to sell? What will give you the best chances for success, or for wild success?

What is the most perfect online product?

The "perfect product" is one that that you and only you sell, and which can be sold and downloaded over the Internet without human intervention. In other words, it's digital information that only you possess, and you are a monopoly. Exquisite – if you can find it! It's elusive for most.

The "least perfect" product is one that is identical to that which is sold by thousands of other sellers. It has no distinguishing characteristics whatsoever. Why should someone buy it from you? Because you are bigger, better, sell cheaper or ship faster? You are located nearby? You provide better service, higher quality? You MUST find or do something unique, and be able to convey it instantly to those shopping in your store, or please, just quit here and save yourself loads of money and time and heartache. You must give people a reason to buy from you.

Most products are somewhere in between the most and least-perfect. Generally, the following formulas apply, though they can be broken by customers for a good reason as you will see:

Product success rankings on the web from *most* to *least* successful

1. **Unique items with no weight and no physical characteristics**: books, information, software that can be delivered by download.
2. **Lightweight and small products** with one or two major characteristics (sight or sound): CD's, books.
3. **Unique items that are of known quality and are purchased by collectors**: art by Thomas Kincaid or Wieland, beanie babies plush toys.
4. **Small items that are repeat purchases**: same size and style of athletic shoes, vitamins, office supplies.
5. **Unique items that have been previously seen in person** and the buyer simply uses the website to complete the purchase: original art, custom goods.
6. **Unique items that must be touched or felt to be trusted**: clothing by an unknown maker or designer.
7. **Goods of undeterminable quality or condition**: second-hand clothing.
8. **Low-density, low-priced commodity items** have a poor break-even ratio: dog food, baby diapers.
9. **Heavy and bulky products**: furniture, weightlifting sets.

You may be able to overcome resistance to your type of goods by offering free samples by mail, a liberal return policy, a free 30 day trial, or other method.

If I build it, will they come?

Your open source commerce store is like the plans for a fabulous building being offered to you for free. You can build it, but if nobody can find you, you might as well not be in business.

Your website is only one of millions and millions that are unknown and still unvisited. I'm sorry, it's not like a unique "Field of Dreams" where you are the only one for hundreds of miles so they must come to you. People will not come just because you build it. Visitors will need a **good reason to visit your store,** and they will give you **less than 10 seconds of their life for you to convince them to stay**. That's like poking their head in the door, doing a quick scan of your store, and then saying "thanks" before you can even say "Hello!"

About 80% of website visits are due to search engine referrals. So getting registered with search engines is one of the most important things you can do to get people into your store. See the chapter on **marketing, advertising and search engines** for help in getting folks to come, OR contact your technical pro and have them do it for you.

The online sales process

Anyone who wants to run an online store needs to do everything that the owner of a physical store would do. This includes:

1. A location or website with a description and pictures of your products or services.
2. A way to let customers know about you and get customers TO your website (i.e. search engines).
3. A way to receive questions from customers and to reply to them.
4. A way for customers to select the products they want, pay for their products, and tell you where they want the products shipped.
5. A way for you to know (receive an email that tells you) when you receive an order.

6. A way to check your list of orders, print invoices or packing lists
7. A way to print postage and shipping labels.
8. A way to notify customers that their order has been shipped.
9. A way for you to track the status of orders.
10. A way to email customers with information about your store or new products.

While there are many, many "shopping cart" programs out there, they only do one of the items above – Item 4. You would still need to find all of the other 9 items or have them custom-programmed for you. THIS is why these open source commerce programs are so amazing. It's all in ONE program.

Getting help: fulfillment, warehousing, shipping services, etc.

Just as many open source commerce stores are installed by a team of specialists working together, many open source commerce stores are run by a team of specialists. I am going to call them your "web services companies." They are as follows:

- **Your local PC Technician.** Every open source commerce store owner needs a local PC Technician they can call on and get quick help to keep their store up and running. Every personal computer is a unique combination of programs and hardware working together in combinations that may never have been tested, so any program can develop a conflict with another. They will set up your anti-virus, anti-spyware, and backup systems so your risks are minimized.

- **Web Hosting Company.** Your website needs to be located on a computer that anyone can access at any time. It should specialize in open source commerce hosting with secure (encrypted) servers, have automatic backups, disaster prevention plans, and continuous technical support. This is not the cheapest hosting available, but would you really locate a physical store at the cheapest location you could find, and expect to make all the money you can? I thought not. Location, location, location. This means a great hosting company.

- **A Store Administrator.** This person (often the store owner) answers pre- and post-purchase customer enquiries. They may also process orders as they come in, prints shipping labels, changes the purchase status to "Shipped" They also check the stock levels and reorder products and packaging (boxes), shipping labels, and postage.

- **A Fulfillment Company.** In a further division of labor, if your store grows quickly you may wish to divest yourself of the burden of warehousing and shipping. A fulfillment company can receive order reports from you, stock and reorder products and packaging (boxes), shipping labels, and postage. See Appendix D for more info.

- **Pack and Ship Company** . If you are not ready for full-on fulfillment and warehousing services, you may work out an arrangement with a local pack and ship company. You bring your products with a list of customer addresses to a company such as Mailboxes Etc., and they carefully wrap, box, label and ship for you. They provide the packaging and materials, so this may be a good intermediate step. See Appendix D for more info.

Online ordering of packaging, shipping supplies

There is no reason to run down to the local office supply store when they will deliver it to your door. Factor in the value of your time and gas, plus free delivery if you purchase $50 or more at a time, and it's a no-brainer.

Office Max, Office Depot and other large office supply stores offer excellent shipping and packaging supplies in quantities of 100 or more at deep discounts. Get an online account and you don't have to stand up.

Getting your postage online

You'll never stand in line the post office again once you open an account and supplies from an online postal services company like Stamps.com. Your postal carrier will love you because your postage is always accurate to 1/10 of a pound with their digital scales. You can add your logo and address to the shipping label so in one sheet it is: your Ship-To address, Ship-From address, the stamp itself, your postage receipt, your logo and any rubber stamp memos you wish to add. What a deal!

6

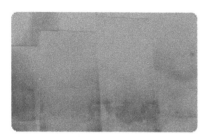

Before you start your online store

If you have an existing store, or once you have decided on a product to sell, you have many decisions, application to make and accounts to open. Your technical pro will need the answers to these questions before they can start working on your store.

Corporate business decisions

If you don't already have an existing company, but are starting a new one, you will need to get or figure out the following:

- What company name will you use? (**TIP**: If you haven't selected a company name yet, make sure the matching DOMAIN NAME is available first)
- Company format: sole proprietorship, partnership, corporation or other?
- Where will you get a logo? Someone local, online logo shop?
- Where will you get business cards?
- Does your business require registration or licensing?

- Are you required to pay tax on sales?
- Are you required to file a D/B/A ("Doing Business As") filing in your city?

Online business decisions to make before you start your store

- What domain name will you use?
- Who will process your credit cards?
- What shipping companies will you use?
- What kind of privacy policy will you have?
- Will you require special conditions of use? For example, are the purchasers of your products required to have a medical, legal or other professional license?
- What kind of shipping boxes will you use? Sizes? Source?
- How much do each of your products weigh?
- Where will you get photos of your products?

You can get help with these decisions in the Cheatsheets in <u>Appendix C</u>.

7

Finding and working with a technical pro

Even the most advanced technical folks have a technical pro they can call on. Here is how to find one and get the most out of that relationship.

Open source commerce programs are powerful, but all that power is not directly accessible to all users. It is constructed with the assumption that you will have a technical pro you can call on.

 TIP: Think of your open source commerce program like a powerful racecar. YOU are the driver, and your technical pro is your racing mechanic. Together you are the racing team.

Do you already have a technical pro?

If you were given this book or told to purchase it by the person who set up your store, congratulations. You are so lucky! You don't have to look any farther to find the right person to help you – you will simply contact them whenever you don't understand something.

How do I find a technical pro of my own?

Your technical pro may be a webmaster, a local consultant, or an employee at the company that hosts your store.

If you don't have any of those, I recommend that you locate a web host that specializes in open source commerce hosting, then call them to see what kind of support they offer. Some hosts are happy to answer any and all questions you may have; others charge a fee, and still others don't want to answer any questions at all.

It is a huge mistake to tell yourself, "but I paid for a year of cheap hosting in advance, so I can't switch to a new host for a year, even though the new host specializes in open source commerce and offers FREE unlimited technical support."

Let's look at the "big picture" here.

Your host that does NOT specialize in open source commerce hosting may cost you $100 for the year, but you may also pay thousands of dollars to a consultant to look up the answers for you! Or, you can let the new open source commerce host move your account FOR you for free, and then all your unlimited technical questions are free.

I personally prefer to go with the **experts who know this program forwards and backwards and can answer my questions immediately.** And believe me, I ask a lot of questions.

A list of web hosts who specialize in open source commerce web hosting is included in Appendix A.

How can I tell if a technical pro is right for me?

You need to find a technical pro that is available during your normal business hours, and who is responsive using the method that YOU are most comfortable with.

I recommend attempting to contact them during YOUR normal business hours, and using your preferred method.

This means that if you are a **"telephone person"** who prefers to grab the phone and call someone, you want to find a technical pro who answers their phone (or at least returns voicemails).

On the other hand, if you are an **Instant Messaging** or **Chat** fool, don't call—you want to find a guru who likes to communicate the same way you do.

If you are the kind of person who simply must talk face to face, you will greatly limit the pool of highly skilled techies who can help you. Many techies work over the Internet and never meet their clients face to face. For all you know, they could be an alien from outer space.

It doesn't matter as long as the two of you can communicate well with each other.

What do I ask my potential technical pro?

Once you make contact, you need to explain exactly what you want from your store. Most techies do NOT read between the lines. They will listen to your words, and be very responsive to exactly what you say, not what you mean.

- **Find out how they charge and what is included.** Ask if the price is negotiable, especially if for some reason your store will be less work than others. Flat-rate pricing is best for you if you know exactly what is included and how long it will take.

- **Do they use a standard contract and project schedule?** A contract is to your mutual benefit. If they don't have one, then you should ask if you can have one drawn up. You may think that what you want and what they will provide is obvious, but in fact it is a zillion shades of gray. Defining your responsibilities and theirs, and what happens if things go wrong is the purpose of a contract. Your lawyer will have to do this for you.

- **How do they handle additions or changes to the project?** There is much you don't know yet about your store and your customers' needs. You will learn this as you go, and then you will want to make adjustments. It is your techie's job to contain the project and make sure it is successfully launched. Techies who allow a project to run on and expand indefinitely are not doing you a favor, they are increasing your chance of failure. If they say that they try to postpone additions until after testing, acceptance, and launch, then that is to your benefit.

- **Ask them how busy they really are right now.** Are they 100% booked already, or will they really have time for you and your needs? Many customers wrongly assume that a programmer can take on an infinite number of projects at a time, and can get their project done in a very short period of time. The fact is, if they are successful, they probably had a full load of customers before you contacted them. Rather than starting your project "now," ask to have your project scheduled to start at a time when they are not fully booked or over-booked. You have a lot of other content development to do first anyway, see below. NOTE: if you do not fully disclose your needs at the beginning and your project runs way over the original time projection, the techie may again become over-booked at the end of the project.

- **See if the payment schedule matches the progress of the project.** You will need to pay a deposit, plus regular progress payments. If the project is two months, you wish to pay 1/3 to start, 1/3 after a month of satisfactory progress, and the final 1/3 when it is done. This gives your techie incentive to finish the project promptly and protects you from paying for more work than they have completed. It also makes it easier on you to spread out payments, since you don't get whomped with a huge bill at the end. Most techies will be flexible on this if you explain your rationale. If they ask for 100% up front, they may have been burned and have a poor view of users. Be wary.

- **Ask to see their online portfolio of other open source commerce stores**. Then afterwards go to the actual stores online to see how they are functioning. Be aware that the store owner may have made changes since launch, and the techie cannot control that. If there are problems in the live store, ask your techie what caused it.

- **See if they will give you a list of references.** If not, that's a very bad sign. They may have plenty of experience but in a slew of never-finished projects. Listen to how they communicate. Most web projects go bad through poor communication.

- **Ask them how they communicate best with their clients—** phone, email, fax, other. You want someone who is willing to communicate the way you do best.

- **Ask about training and instruction.** If you want them to teach you everything they know, you must tell them. Some techies love to explain things, others just want to program.

- **Find out who will create your product pages.** You, or the techie? If you have a large number of products, you may submit that information to them for them to upload in one batch. If you have a small number of products, you may want to ask your techie to do a few examples and you type the rest yourself.

- **Do you want a turn-key project?** If you want them to do it all and you just collect the money as it rolls in, tell them that, too.

- **Will they give you a project schedule and weekly progress reports?** These are your best ways to keep a project moving along.

- **Do they have a designated backup or assistant you can contact if they are not available?** Many techies work independently, but like doctors they should always have a designated person you can contact in case of an emergency. If not, you may be left out in the cold if they get sick or go on vacation or to Belize.

If they can't do what you want, don't worry. Most techies will be happy to refer you to someone who can.

As long as you take responsibility for communicating exactly what you want with a techie, you will get it. The responsibility lies upon you.

 TIP: Remember, most web projects go bad through poor communication. Answering the above questions BEFORE you start can prevent most of these issues.

8

Managing your website project

Now that you have found your techie, you have lots of non-technical project management decisions to make.

Where to start?

So you've found a technical pro who's agreed to lead you through the wilderness of your first store. That's great! Now the fun begins. Both you and your techie have lots of things to do, so the sooner you get going on them, the better.

How long will it take?

The length of an open source commerce store development project depends on how long it takes for you to make decisions and how long it takes for you to develop the content that goes on the pages. It's a lot like building a home. If you know what you want, it can go quickly. If you change your mind a lot, it will take that much longer.

Theoretically, you could have a store up and running in about thirty minutes if you knew exactly what you want. I have done this myself, but it was a website for me so I knew exactly what to do. In reality, most stores take anywhere from 30 to 60 days because of waiting for decisions from you, the dear customer, and waiting for you to make the many little decisions that add up to a website. If you use all my checklists and cheatsheets and templates that are available in this book and on the web, then your project can go at lightning speed.

I like to tell my clients that whether you hurry or whether you go slow, it takes six weeks to open the doors of a website. If you hurry too much, you end up re-making decisions or making them too quickly. If you go slow, you give yourself a little time to think over each decision. Ironically, the more a client is in a terrible hurry, I have found that he is less likely to actually finish his website.

How much will it cost?

Just like rushing or going methodically gets you there about the same time, an open source commerce store is pretty predictable in the cost as well. You can do it all yourself, very slowly, make many mistakes but also learn about every part; or you can hire a pro who can do it efficiently the first time. If you add up the cost of your own labor, credit card processing application fees, setup fees, designer or template, etc., it will be several thousand dollars of your time or your cash, no matter which method you use.

How much should you customize?

I recommend for your first store that you decide on a simple to moderate design or template, and then stay with it. Don't go for something really fancy that may or may not be attainable. The more complicated it is, the more likely it is to fail. You want to ensure success. Stick with simple.

Your role

Your main role is to communicate your wants clearly, in a way that can be understood and acted upon.

- Contact your technical pro well before you need to. Don't wait until *after* a deadline has passed.
- Use the communication channels that you agreed to, whether phone, fax, or carrier pigeon. If you agree on email, he or she will not hear the phone.
- Establish clear schedules and expectations. When they will contact you, if ever. More likely you will contact them.
- Use clear, precise language to get the best response from your techie. See the "What You Say" chart below for help.

Unlike many fields where tact or courtesy is valued, your techie will appreciate your *total directness and honesty*. Any words that modify or diminish your directness will hinder your project and its success.

Your techie's role

Your techie will respond to your needs when you state them, and will take action after you have provided enough information. It is impossible for him or her to proceed without information that you need to give, and if it's impossible, they don't.

Programming Efficiency

There is a lot of invisible overhead time involved in programming an open source commerce site, i.e. time setting everything up and opening the many programs they need open at once, finding all your passwords, etc. Your techie will NOT do this each time you trickle ONE piece of information to them, or they will quickly go out of business. They will save it up until the information you have sent reaches critical mass, and they have verified that they completely understand what you mean. ONLY THEN will they efficiently program all you've sent in one sitting.

Maximizing communications

Learn a little Tech-Speak in order to maximize your effectiveness during the building of your store. Here are some examples:

What you say:	What a techie hears:
I sure would like...	Blah, blah, blah
I want or I need...	I want or I need...
Hi, please call me, bye.	Blah, blah blah blah, blah.
I need to talk to you about X	I need to talk to you about X
I sure do hope I can get this real soon.	Blah blah blah blah blah blah blah blah blah.
The deadline is Friday.	The deadline is Friday.
Ahhh! Help! It's gone! I pushed some button and my website disappeared! Oh my gosh, I can't believe I did that! Ahh!	Blah! Blah! Blah, blah! Blah blah blah blah blah blah blah blah blah! Blah blah blah, blah blah blah, blah blah, blah! Blah!
I clicked the "Delete" button and error message "Error 12345" came up and the website disappeared.	I clicked the "Delete" button and error message "Error 12345" came up and the website disappeared.

Please don't think the purpose of the above is to disparage techies at all. You may not have dealt with technical people before with YOUR money on the line. Read it over and over until you fully get the hang of it.

TIP: Your techie will NOT get his or her feelings hurt when YOU feel you are being extremely blunt. They WILL get annoyed if you "beat around the bush" and don't say exactly what you mean so they have to do the work several times.

Your project schedule

It's important for you to work out a project schedule AND for you to check to make sure that each milestone has been reached to your satisfaction AS it is reached. Every new store owner has some fear perhaps of learning a new program, and seems to drag their feet a little about logging on and looking at what your techie has done. DO NOT DELAY. Each day that you assume that it's fine is a day that the project gets a little more entrenched in that direction. HOPING that it's going the right direction is not enough. You must see the progress (or regress) with your eyes.

Weekly progress reports

The best way to keep your project on track is to get a weekly – say Monday – report from your techie on what was accomplished the week before. Techies generally like reporting on Mondays, because they can work all weekend to catch up if things get crazy, and they can still happily report to you on Monday that everything is on schedule.

Phases of an open source commerce website project

All web projects including open source commerce go through these four phases: **design, programming, testing, acceptance,** and **launch**. You will need to give your input at every phase.

How much time to devote to each phase?

Your typical open source commerce project schedule will be about **1/3 design, 1/3 programming, and 1/3 for testing, acceptance, product data entry, and launch.** In a six week project, that's two weeks for each phase. This is enough time for you to thoroughly ponder the decisions required of each decision.

What happens during the Design phase?

This is where you describe exactly what you want your store to look like and your techie makes it so. Many techies can either do graphic design well OR they can program well, but it is rare for them to do both well. One is right-brain activity, the other is left-brain, and you know how rare it is for a person to use their whole brain.

The point is that your techie may rely on a graphic designer to do the actual design for you, or they may do it themselves. Either way, I will call this person the designer for this phase of the project.

Your logo is the design starting point

The starting point for most store designs is your store's logo. If you have a logo, great, move onto the next section. Some designers do logos; many do not. If not, ask them for a referral to a logo designer.

You may think that designing or deciding on a logo would easy and fun. Wait until you see the first set of logo mockups and you will realize it is an exercise fraught in hidden meanings and symbolism. "Red is a strong color and means luck in Asia" "It looks too much like a stop sign" "It's too soft" "It's too trendy" "It's just …not me."

Moreover, a logo must not only look good on a website, but also printed in black and white on a copier and across a variety of media. It must be easily recognizable and not confusingly similar to other logos (which may also be protected trademarks or service marks).

Design Mockups

Before your designer starts designing your store, it is best if you can decide on the general style of logo you want (bold or soft, rounded or angular, contemporary or traditional, etc) and the color you prefer. If they do design logos, you will be way ahead of the game, and if they do not, they can still proceed with the design using a placeholder.

Some designers write a detailed description of what you want and include that in your contract. Others listen to your description of what you want and create a store design for you (called a "mock-up") directly in a graphics program like PhotoShop, attaching that to your contract.

 TIP: Be sure to find out in advance what happens if you don't like a design mockup. Will they modify it an unlimited number of times? Will they create a different one for your approval? Do you pay for both designs, or just the one you choose?

Your website mock-up will look like a photograph of a website, but of course you can't click any links and nothing actually works. Make sure it is as close as possible to what you want, because your designer will slice and dice that picture and your techie will use those images in your actual website.

Remember, like a mouth-watering picture of a cake on a cake box, your store mockup is an artist's conception of a website – like a "serving suggestion" picture of a delicious recipe.

Your techie may need to make some changes to the design, such as reducing the size of some images, to make the pages load faster. It's a balancing act between beauty and function. But your website will be substantially similar to your original design.

What happens during the Programming phase?

Once you've okayed the design, you can breathe a sigh of relief as the designer hands over the graphics and your techie takes over.

In this phase, you will need to provide a lot of "content" to the programmer to program. Think of content as the "words on the page." For example, the text that is unique to the Home page, to a "Shipping & Returns Policy" page, or to a "Frequently Asked Questions" page.

What pages do you want? That depends on your product and what the buyer needs to know to understand your product. If your product is a no-brainer that everyone understands, then you don't need "Frequently Asked Questions." If people ask you the same questions about it over and over, well, you can prevent many of those questions with an FAQ.

You will be able to add pages later as the need develops or as your understanding of what your online customers need to do business with you. That is the beauty of a website – unlike print, where it has to be perfect the first time, a website can grow and change as often as you wish.

Your programmer should give you a schedule that lists when you need to provide content for each page to them. If not, you'd better ask what date they need it by or your project may grind to a halt.

Even if you meet with your techie face to face, you should provide everything by email or other electronic format. Please don't give or fax them hand-written pieces of paper, it is too inaccurate. Proof your work BEFORE you submit it because it simply bogs down the project for them to correct your mistakes after you give it to them.

Your techie will take your content and remove all the formatting so it is text-only. Then they will paste the text into the HTML web page and use

HTML codes to make it look as similar as possible to your original formatting.

Here is a list of all the information you need to provide to your techie before your store will be ready to program (note, all of these items are available in Appendix C):

Pre-Setup Checklist – What colors do you want? What size and style of font? 52 nitty gritty items that your installer might otherwise have to ask you one at a time. Charts for colors, font sizes and styles. A copy of my Pre-Setup Checklist is included as Appendix A, or, you may fill out my online checklist and have the results mailed to you or your techie.

Product Information - Product descriptions, photos, model number, weight, package size for some shippers, quantity in stock. Optional: keywords that people would use if searching for this product in a search engine.

Payment and Shipping Methods – what payments will you accept? Do you want to pay a monthly fee plus a per-transaction charge, or would you rather pay a percentage of every transaction? How will you ship to customers – postal service, UPS, FedEx, other methods? Start with one, you can add more later. Right now you just need to decide what methods to offer, and inform your techie.

Customizations - One of the coolest things about open source commerce is that when anyone makes a custom program for their store, they donate it back to the community. So you don't have to reinvent the wheel; if you want to tweak your store, chances are someone else has already done that and their add-on or 'contribution' is available for free.

Some add-ons are not included in the standard open source commerce but are really nice or even necessary. For example, you must have password protection for your private administration pages, otherwise anybody could add or remove products, get a backup copy of your database, etc.

When your techie is programming your store, it is important for them to install the most complicated add-on first, then the next-most complicated, and so forth. This saves them a lot of time and headaches, and saves you money too. Of course they can always be added later, but it's a Very Good Idea to decide beforehand on as many as you can.

There is an add-on contribution for just about anything that you can dream up. Someone has done it before. So think it up, ask your techie to see if it's out there, and give it a try.

Information Boxes – The information boxes in the left and right columns. You can customize the headings, and wordings in each box. The InfoBoxes checklist listed in Appendix C goes through every box on the site from top to bottom and left to right, making sure you are satisfied with the wording and contents of each one.

Greetings and Menu Bars - Hello, Guest! Do you like being greeted like this? Most open source commerce programs say this when a visitor has not yet registered for an account in your store. You can change the wording of greetings to suit your tastes, or even remove them completely. You can also change the wording of the top menu bars to whatever you wish. There is a cheat sheet listed in Appendix C that goes through every greeting and menu bar, making sure you are satisfied with the wording and contents of each one.

Your Privacy Policy - Privacy laws in many countries require that you inform customers of how the information you collect about them – name, email address, etc. – exactly how that information will be used, whether you will sell or rent it to third parties, etc. The wording of this policy depends upon what you plan to do with the information, and it is important that you have your lawyer review and approve your privacy policy.

Your Shipping & Returns Policy - Many customers will not buy from you unless you have a stated shipping & returns policy that explains exactly how you charge for shipping and how you handle returns. Customers do not like to be surprised at the end of check-out with high unexplained shipping fees or that you ship only to a country or area where they do not live.

Your Payment Methods Policy - It is important to offer several alternative payment methods. Many customers will not buy from you unless you state in advance exactly what payments you accept. Customers do not like to be surprised at the end of check-Out to find out that you only accept a certain credit card!

Your Customer Emails - Every open source commerce store has a standard Welcome email that is sent to customers when they first register, and an Order Receipt email that is sent after a customer purchases from you. Other minor emails are sent when a customer loses or changes their password. Customize these to provide a high level of customer service.

 TIP: To see these emails – register as a customer, order a test product, and then check your inbox!

Once you have completed all of the above and submitted them to your techie, you may think you can sit back and wait for your store to be built. But it can be a huge mistake if you don't monitor the progress on a regular basis!

What happens during the Testing phase?

When your techie tells you that the draft site is ready, it is time for you to take it for a real "test drive." You must experience your store the same way that your customers will. You may not know a lot about your customers yet, but you can probably make some educated guesses that you can refine later. Here are the items you will need to know in order to thoroughly test your store:

Will your customers have:

- Large computer screens or small?
- Slow internet connections or fast?
- What browser – Internet Explorer, Netscape, Mozilla or other?
- What country –your country only, selected other countries, all countries?

Before you make your store you will have to make educated guesses at this information, but later on your techie can get reports for you that tell you this information and more.

Should you enlist friends or family to help test your store?

It is a good idea to enlist your friends and family in your testing venture. To do this, I would create a pretend product that costs $1.00 and give each friend or family member some money to "spend" in your store. Have them report to you their screen size, internet connection speed, browser, etc. and the results of their purchase.

Any comments from your family and friend testers have will be extremely important, because once you open your shop, regular customers will not be so forthcoming with their suggestions or feedback. But remember: if your friend or relative has a very different profile than your expected customers (for example, way more or less experienced than your average customer), then you should weigh their feedback accordingly.

Your techie will have run some test orders through your website before he or she gives it to you, but you need to know that REAL orders are working well. You will want to sign up as a customer and buy some products, and fully check out. This way you will receive all the "customer emails" that your other customers will receive. If there is anything you don't like, you must say so now, not a few weeks after the launch.

Likewise, YOU must look at every single page of your website with your own eyes. It's like walking around your store. This includes your "Privacy statement," "Shipping & returns," every product, and any other pages you have.

Communicating Changes

Take notes of the wording and if you don't like it, send a list of things to change to your techie and copy the exact page address from your browser (or else your techie will have to reply each time "What page are you talking about?" to verify what you mean).

Address   http://www.yourwebsite.com/apage.php?info&asdfjfdgafdg

Highlight this whole address and select EDIT – COPY, then in your email below select EDIT – PASTE so he or she knows the exact page you want to change.

Subject: Changes for my website:

1. On page product_info.php?cPath=1&products_id=8 change "One size fits all" to "One size fits most."
2. On page product_info.php?cPath=5&products_id=17 remove the product picture and replace with the attached picture, PRODUCT17.png
3. On page information.php?info_id=3 Please remove the last paragraph.

If you need to send more requests (and it is best if you can keep ALL changes in one email but sometimes that is not possible), start your next message using the same numbering system. So if you sent the above 3 changes the first time, your second message will look like this:

Subject: Additional Changes for my website:

4. On page product_info.php?cPath=1...
5. On page product_info.php?cPath=5...

This way you can test and check off each item when your techie says they are done AND you have tested them; when all the numbers are crossed out, your website is done!

What happens during product data entry phase?

If your store has many products, you may provide all of your product information to your techie in a spreadsheet so he or she could "dump" it all at once into your store. This is done using an add-in called "EasyPopulate" because it easily fills ("populates") your store. If so, product data entry is just one upload of the spreadsheet and another upload of all your product photos.

If you don't have a lot of products though, you may be entering them yourself as described in the Jump Start Guide. Often your techie will enter several for you as an example, or they may bid separately on doing this, or you may do it. Each store and project is different.

What happens during the Acceptance phase?

Acceptance is when you formally tell your techie that you have looked at and/or tested each part of your store, and you agree that he or she has done everything they agreed to do. Be sure to pull out your contract and read every word; don't trust your memory.

 TIP: A website is never done, there is always "just one more thing" to do to it before it is finished. Learn to live with this feeling, it is normal.

Unlike publishing a book or brochure, there is not a firm deadline where it ALL has to be done or else, and it is set in ink and published and done. This is the beauty and the curse of websites. The beauty is that you can always do one more thing. The curse is that you always have the feeling that you *should* do one more thing.

Your final payment to your techie signifies that you have accepted their work and are ready to launch. Don't make this payment if you are sure something is still not done. Once you make this payment, any additional changes you want will be billed separately.

What happens during Launch phase?

For launch, once your techie verifies that they have received payment, they will remove the "Coming Soon!" page that has been hiding your site from curious visitors' eyes. Your site is officially launched, visible for all the world to see! It's also time to tell search engines that you are ready for business and to start marketing and advertising, but that is covered in a later chapter.

What do I do if things go wrong?

Don't worry, it is inevitable in *any* project that something will go wrong, whether large or small. It's probably due to your messy human communication style, but whatever. The longer the project, the more likely that sticky, messy human life issue will intervene.

 TIP: Every project has some problems, the only question is how you will deal with it.

You need to communicate this problem to your techie calmly and factually. This will maximize your chances of a quick and successful resolution.

DO NOT GRAB THE PHONE in a panic and start babbling hysterically; they cannot process your hysteria and YOU cannot think clearly. You must get PAST your hysteria. See the above chart for what happens when you babble. Wait until you are calm and can state what happened 1, 2, 3. Then call.

 TIP: Your brain must get over the hysteria before it can figure out what went wrong.

Reporting a problem to your techie:

Don't bring your feelings into it, use facts only. Whether you were surprised or scared is just noise to your techie.

State exactly what you did when something happened. Don't fudge. Don't say "I think it was…"

Write down the error message you saw. DO NOT GUESS. DO NOT PARAPHRASE OR SUMMARIZE. This error message tells your techie how to solve your problem. WITHOUT IT THEY CANNOT HELP YOU.

Tell EXACTLY what you have already done to try to solve it. Otherwise your techie will have to suggest each thing that you have already done before you can make any progress, and this will only frustrate both of you.

Finding other sources of tech help

Your techie may get an extended illness, suffer a disability, have a relative die, or go to Belize for a few months. The longer your project drags on, the more likely this will occur.

If this happens, it is always best if you can **ask them for a referral to someone who can finish the project.**

If this is impossible, for example if they turned off their phone for the months that they are in Belize, you may have to try other sources. See Appendix A for more help.

TIP: Most techies will not work on a store someone else started; that is like tracking down an intermittent electrical problem on your car. It is cheaper for you if they start with a fresh, clean, pure, and predictable installation of open source commerce.

For help and moral support after your store is launched, join an email group of people like you, oscommerce-newbies@yahoogroups.com. Just click this link and send the email that pops up - you don't even need to fill in the subject line, unless you insist.

9

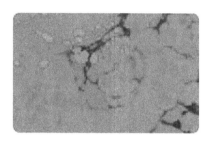

Opening day!

Your techie has just sent you an email saying that your new website has been launched. It's show time! Woo hoo! You are probably staring at your brand-new store wondering what the heck you do now. The first thing to do is check your store to see that it really truly is live.

Is it there? Good! Now you find out what you're really getting into. Except that nobody knows where you are, so like most new businesses, whether on the web or not, your store will be empty a great deal of the time until you can entice customers to come and fill it up.

This will take traditional marketing methods as well as search engine magic. Email your friends and family, tell them to tell all of THEIR friends, offer new customer discounts to get people to try your store or run coupons in your local paper. Anything you'd do in a regular store, you can do with your online store!

What do I do first?

Turn to the Jump Start Guide and run through that, see if there's anything you want to do. Every store owner wants to change a word on their main page, look at new orders, change a product description, add a new product photo, add another page or change the wording on some pages.

How do you know when you have customers?

 TIP: You can see the people are in your store and find out a bit about each of them by going to your Admin panel and clicking TOOLS – WHO'S ONLINE.

You will probably know that you have your first potential customer by receiving a question by email from your Contact Us page. Until it is obvious that your store is active (i.e. many reviews, bestseller list, high page count on your bottom bar that says "total visitors since [starting date]"), many people who want to buy from you will first test you by asking a question.

Your first sale!

If you reply promptly to customer inquiries, with good customer service manners, then they will decide that your store is active and not malicious and they may often purchase within minutes of receiving your answer.

 TIP: Getting your store's first real sale is an exciting moment in your store's history! Be sure to celebrate so you always remember that day.

Many customers will also contact you with what appears to be a complaint (why don't you order X? why doesn't this product come in extra-large?). This is simply another way that they test you to make sure you will be responsive to their needs, and to make sure that you are not malicious or not really in business.

Take these possible complaints seriously and respond kindly, especially if two people suggest the same thing. Each suggestion is a possible way to improve your website. If you don't, you are losing possible sales with each suggestion or complaint you ignore.

Getting "return customers"

Many people do not buy the first time they visit an online store. They may even sign up for an account the first time, but buy nothing. They want to consider their purchase carefully. You can make your store as enticing as possible to these valuable return visitors by keeping the text on your home page fresh and new. Add or subtract news, change the wording! It's like putting up displays in a store window to attract peoples' eyes.

When do you know you are out of start-up mode?

If you continue to be responsive and kind to customers when they inquire, change your home page regularly, one day you may find that the complaints are gone, your store is working smoothly, and you have nothing left to work on. That is when you know you are out of start-up mode.

10

Running your store day-to-day

If you remember to think of yourself as a manager of a regular store, just like a store on the street corner, everything you do to manage your store in open source commerce will seem easy and normal.

 TIP: Your open source commerce store will eventually mature to two things: shipping, and customer service.

Start your day with good customer service

Since your customers can shop around the clock, start your day by immediately checking and replying to enquiries. It's as if when you walk in the door there is a huddle of customers at the counter asking you questions. They're from different time zones, so they may have been waiting a while.

TIP: Dealing with Difficult People. Remember to think of your store like a restaurant: the people who enter are hungry for your goods, and may be easily upset until they are full. These people may also become your best and most grateful customers.

 TIP: You have one goal in customer service: to earn and keep the TRUST of your customers and potential customers. With no trust, you will have NO business.

Developing trust with your customers

Trust begins with your prompt and courteous response to feedback sent from your Contact Us page. Enquiries from this page will fall into the following categories:

1. **Pre-sales inquiries:** Those who do not trust that your store is actively in business and need to see your timely and trustworthy response before they will buy.
2. **Special requests:** Those who want or need you to make a special accommodation before they can/will order from you. You should not automatically trust all these requests, as some scammers may try to leverage your trust with this method.
3. **Ordering problems:** Those who trust your store enough to try to buy, but ran into unexpected problems which have mildly breached their sense of trust. These customers are highly motivated to buy IF you can overcome their problem in a timely manner.
4. **Post-purchase inquiries:** Those who have given you their trust and need reassurance of your performance. You should be able to prevent most of these inquiries by empowering the customer with the information they need to track the status of their purchase on their own.
5. **Repeat customer or volume discount inquiries:** Some customers are from cultures that expect discounts or special treatment as a result of your relationship with them. You should either keep a

nominal discount offer on hand for such situations or develop a kind but firm policy against it.

6. **Gift or charity requests:** Some visitors will ask for your product for free because they are a student or poor or for some other good cause. Whether you choose to consider their requests for the public relations value or choose to refuse all requests, develop a policy for it.

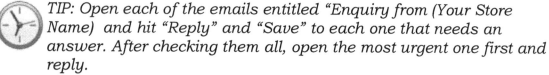

TIP: Open each of the emails entitled "Enquiry from (Your Store Name) and hit "Reply" and "Save" to each one that needs an answer. After checking them all, open the most urgent one first and reply.

TIP: Your Computer Tech Support person can set up your computer's email program so that emails relating to your store go into a separate Store folder.

This way you won't have to sift through dozens and dozens of spams to get to these critical messages, and you can quickly reply within your first hour of the business day.

Processing Emails

The three main types of emails relating to your store which should go into this email folder are:

1. **Enquiries from the Contact Us** page with the subject, "Enquiry from your store" or the subject line you have had your technical pro change it to. These will typically run the gamut from pre-sales inquiries or complaints about your store, to current customers following up on their order to see whether it has shipped or requests for returns, exchanges or refunds. If you sell a technical product, you will also receive requests for support here.

2. **A copy of the order receipt emails** that your store sends to each customer when they successfully place an order. The default

subject line for this receipt is "Order Process." If the subject says ""RE: Order Process" it means a customer has sent an enquiry to you by replying to their store receipt. Treat this like a special enquiry.

3. **A copy of the credit card email receipt**s your credit card processor sends to your customer when they place an order, and any other messages you may receive from your credit card processor.

 TIP: Save a text document with the various things you say to customers over and over, said in the very best and most polite way. Save it to your Desktop as "Snippets" so you can access it repeatedly throughout the day.

Check orders – sort pending orders

You have already glanced at all your orders in your email box as you checked enquiries, but that is only part of the information. Now you need to log onto your store to process the order, get the details, and change their order status to shipped.

Open your web browser, type in the address for your store's Admin area, and log on. Click the **"Orders"** link to see the list of your most recent Orders.

 TIP: You can easily sort this list of orders so it temporarily displays only all the Pending, Processing, or Shipped orders. Simply click the STATUS box in the top right of your page.

 TIP: Click the Edit icon to the left of the customer's name to jump directly into that customer's order.

Make shipping labels

You will want to buy nice shipping labels to make your business look professional. Use the template that comes packaged with that shipping label to set them up so they are properly aligned. If you need to call your printer's support department to get them to line up right, do it.

 TIP: Buy your shipping labels and other shipping supplies online – save gas and time.

Copy the first shipping address for the first order by highlighting it and selecting CTRL-C or by clicking the top menu EDIT-COPY. Then PASTE this (CTRL-V or EDIT-PASTE) into a Word document that's set up to print your labels.

On the line above the customer's name, copy the Order Number, Date, and Product Model Number. This will make it easy to fulfill and double-check your orders later.

Change order status

After you have created the shipping label, go to your Snippets document and copy and paste in the order's "comments" box the appropriate comments, thanking them for the order and telling them that their order is being processed, will go out today or next business day.

Change their order status to "PROCESSING" or "SHIPPED."

Print a packing slip (or invoice if the customer has not yet paid).

Click "UPDATE" and move on to the next order. *An automatic email will be sent to the customer notifying them of the status change, and they will see the comments you just typed in.*

Repeat

Repeat until you have picked up all of today's orders, then go back a day or two further to be sure you didn't miss any orders from the day before.

Now that you have all your orders copied onto shipping labels, you make a duplicate copy of each label. This second shipping label will be pasted to the Delivery Confirmation receipt for US shipments, or to the Customs Declaration form for international shipments. You hit "Print," pull the finished labels off your printer and take them over to your shipping center.

 TIP: You may be able to purchase online postage, and print a shipping and return address label in one smooth operation, bypassing many of these shipping label steps.

If you live in the U.S. you can buy postage online from the U.S. Postal Service. I use Stamps.com because it is much more customer-service oriented (i.e. easier to use). Check to see if this type of service is available in your country.

Package up your orders and ship

Now that you have your shipping labels ready (either manually printed or from an online source like Stamps.com), take all your printed labels and move to your store's shipping center. Here is where you have envelopes in the appropriate different sizes for single and multiple purchases.

Count up the orders, and pull the appropriate envelopes and merchandise to fit.

Affix the label, drop in the merchandise, insert the appropriate packing slip or invoice, and seal the flap.

You still need to affix the delivery confirmation or customs receipt, slap the second shipping label on that, and stamp the package with "Priority Mail" "Air Mail" or other appropriate shipping rate.

 TIP: If possible, to reduce customer enquiries, ship ALL goods with a delivery confirmation and have the tracking number automatically sent to the customer, so they can track the status of their purchase online.

 TIP: When purchased online with postage from Stamps.com, a delivery confirmation is only U.S. thirteen cents.

Finally, **double-check your packages before mailing.** Even if you use self-stick envelopes, they can easily open en route. Tape the flap shut for extra protection. If you don't do this now, you will start after your first customer complains that the envelope was open, and there was no merchandise in it.

Also, if you use an Ink Jet printer as many small businesses do, cover the shipping label with clear tape –they can smear without it.

Check stock levels and office supplies

Whether or not you use the store's inventory level checking, after shipping visually check your stock levels and place re-orders when they reach a pre-set minimum level. Do the same with your address labels, envelopes, etc.

11

Executive management decisions

Dealing with Complaints

No matter how well you run your open source commerce store, you will always receive a certain number of complaints. Some people are just born to complain, others border on fraud because they want to use your product and return it like a prom dress with the tags stuck back on, but some offer very valuable information for improving your store. It is your job to sort them out.

Valuable Feedback

The complaint feedback from most of your customers is valuable, even priceless. Big companies would pay thousands of dollars to focus groups, testers, paid people who may or may not make the same observations as real customers. Any time you can change your website or incorporate a change based on feedback, do it. Especially if two people make the same comment.

Born to Complain

A few people complain about everything. It's too hot, it's too cold, your product is too easy, your product is too hard. You will learn to recognize them because their enquiries contain a lot of vague problems. If you do manage to sort through them and solve them, they will write again with another set of problems, and another. If you stretch a store policy for them, they ask you to stretch another. I call them "black holes" because nothing satisfies them, you keep sinking more and more of your time and resources into it. Every day another message from them greets you. One day if you give up and give them a refund, they will complain about that! Nothing you do will satisfy them. But they are rare.

Stick to your store policies (next section), learn to recognize them early, give them an early refund if you can and move on.

Setting Store Policies

You must set store policies on refunds, shipping, returns, and privacy. According to some authorities, having written policies *and following them exactly* can help in your favor if someone files a lawsuit against you – and remember, anyone can file a lawsuit about anything.

Will you offer refunds, and under what conditions? How will you ship, and how do you select and charge for a shipper? Will you allow customers to return goods, can they be used or must the goods show no wear and have the original tags still on them? How do you use the personal information you collect from your customers – their name, address, phone, etc.? Will you sell it to email marketing lists? Or simply use it to fulfill and contact them about their order?

 TIP: For examples of store policies others have used, use a search engine. Remember they are copyrighted, so you cannot copy them. Check with your attorney to see if the policies you propose will protect you.

Dealing with FRAUD

Most people are honest, but fraud is a problem for every store owner. Depending on the type of merchandise you sell, it may be more or less of a problem. If a customer claims that their credit card was fraudulently used or used without their permission, YOU will be the one who loses.

Recognizing suspicious orders:

You will soon learn to recognize suspicious or possibly fraudulent orders:

- It will be an unusual order, for example, one of everything in your store or an unusually large quantity of one product.
- It will have a free email address
- It will have an email address name that is completely different from the credit card name
- It will have an email address from one country, and a delivery address to another.
- It will have a delivery address that sounds suspiciously like a prison inmate number and address i.e. "Unit #..." (don't laugh, it happened to me)
- Your credit card company will flag it as suspicious, i.e. zip code doesn't match, customer IP address does not match billing & shipping address.

When you receive an order that looks suspicious, contact the purchaser before shipping. Just a simple phone call will very likely tell you if it's real, because most cons will not give away their real phone number – it's too easily traced to them.

If an order is fraudulent, you will have to issue a refund whether you have shipped or not. You lose. It's called the School of Hard Knocks. This should be a rare situation, perhaps once or twice a year if you are vigilant. See if there was anything you can learn about the order that will help you recognize fraud next time, or any policies you should change to protect yourself.

Reporting & planning

All open source commerce stores have reports built-in that are of tremendous strategic value to you.

One strategic report is which products have sold the most. This tells you that the information you have given about this product is adequate to convince people to part with their hard-earned money. Use this product as an example to adjust the information you give about your other products.

Another strategic report is which products people have viewed the most. If they are looking but not buying, you want to find out why for strategic reasons.

- Are you explaining the product well enough to convince them to buy?
- On the other hand, are you making such wild claims that they don't believe how great it is?
- Is the price too high, so people leave to buy the product elsewhere?
- Is the price too low for people to believe that it is of good quality?

- Do you have a good product picture(s) that allows the customer to visualize the product before buying?
- Is the same product available in many other stores at equal or lower price?

Compare this product to the report of products that have sold the most, AND to other stores on the Internet, and make adjustments. Check again in a few weeks to see if it has made a difference.

Who is in your store right now?

"Who's Online?" is a "real-time" report in your private Admin area (click Tools – Who's Online) that gives you some information about the people in your store at the moment you check it. Watch this for a period of time, hitting "Refresh" to see the new information as the visitors move from one area to another!

- Is everyone coming to your Home page and then leaving quickly? You definitely need to beef up the home page or make it seem more credible to visitors.
- Do you have a lot of "Not Found" addresses? Write down the addresses, and ask your techie why.
- Are people spending a lot of time in one particular non-sales area? Should you make that area smaller or funnel them towards your sales area?

Who are your best customers?

Which customers have spent the most money in your store? Treat these Very Important People extra special! Learn to cater to them, ask their opinions, and take them very seriously. They like what you do, and it is benefiting them as well as you.

Other reports

Some versions of open source commerce have other built-in reports, or you can have them added to your store. These include:

Monthly sales/tax report

This report adds up your sales each month and year like an accountant would, and displays it in beautiful columns with gross sales, tax, shipping, gift certificates, etc. displayed. You can download the report and sort and play with it in Excel or other spreadsheet simply by clicking a button.

Detailed custom reporting

Your technical pro can use a program called "phpMyAdmin" to reach into your store's database and create ANY custom report you may want:

- How many customers live in a certain area?
- How many customers purchased more than one product?
- Which customers purchased one product but not another?
- How many customers have created accounts but not made any purchases? Perhaps you can email them a special coupon good for their first purchase.
- Which customers with email addresses ordered a product that you now have an upgrade for? You can notify them or offer the upgrade at a special price.

12

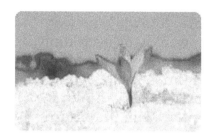

Making a good store even better

Are search engines really that important?

Yes, they are. About 80% of website visits are due to search engine referrals, and about 80% of *those* search engine referrals are from **Google**. So getting registered with search engines is one of the most important things you can do to get people into your store.

What do search engines want?

It changes all the time, so they can keep ahead of spammers and scammers. It used to be your meta tags, but that was so misused that it has changed. Now the content on your home page is considered key: some search engines like Google will only list a keyword if it is *also* found in the text of your home page. Others use different criteria. Some use all lower case (small) letters, others treat capitalized words differently. Some don't care about the order you put them in, others do. No wonder it's confusing.

What does Google want?

Google, the biggest and most popular search engine, "crawls" the web every 28 days looking for and analyzing new sites; weekly or even daily if you have a high-traffic site. If the keyword is also found on your home page, it likes you. If the keyword is found multiple times it likes you even more (up to five of the same word on the page —after that in thinks you might be cheating). If you have many "incoming links" from important and popular websites, Google will list you higher. Incoming links from low-traffic or unpopular sites will get you listed lower. It's just one big popularity contest!

How do you get listed with the search engines?

There is so much hoopla about search engines. You can spend a fortune on "Search engine optimization" and still not get good rankings. There are dirty secrets that most of these experts will not tell you:

Three big, dirty secrets about search engines

Big secret #1 about search engines:

Search engines have programs running all the time, day and night, looking all over the web for new websites. And they are going to find yours eventually. The question is how long it will take.

If you want to grow your store slowly, you *may not need to do a thing to get search engines to find you.* The average time for them to bump into your site is from two weeks to four months. You can test it simply by going to a popular search engine such as Google and typing in the name of your store (Not the address, with a .com after it, but the actual name as written on the pages of your website). I once had a search engine find my site within a day of first starting to put it up, but that is fantastically rare. They work methodically, and they just happened to be on my part of the web when I started the site.

Big secret #2 about search engines:

Only the people who program them know exactly how they work, and that is a confidential trade secret they cannot tell anyone. Everyone else learns by testing them, and making assumptions based on the results. This is why each search engine optimization company says a different thing is most important.

Here's big secret #3 about search engines:

They change their formulas all the time, to try to keep ahead of folks who figure them out and then write automated submission programs. Search engines HATE automated submission programs. Maybe they are worried that automated computers will take over the universe, I don't know. But it sure does keep things lively for the rest of us folks. Submit your site manually by going to each of the major search engines (and you can find a list of them by going to google.com!) and clicking a link like "Submit My Site."

Ten Steps to Set Search Engine "Bait" and get your open source commerce store listed with the major search engines

Doing search engine optimization on your own website is a lot like fishing. You set bait traps that will look enticing to them. This means using an add-on (or a form of open source commerce with the add-on pre-installed) that will allow you to do this.

1. Find yourself a *most important search word.*

Decide what word most people will use when searching for your store. We will call this your **main keyword.**

 TIP: Use this main keyword as much as possible on your website, up to 5 times on a web page or you may be accused of spamming the word.

2. Brainstorm a list of other important search words people might use looking for your store

Type them in an email or word processor (TOOLS – WORD COUNT) and delete extras until you have 1,000 characters of good search words.

 TIP: Think up keywords until you have 1,000 characters of good search words Type them in an email then select TOOLS – WORD COUNT to see total word and character count.

3. Make sure your store's title is not "osCommerce" (or the name of your program) and that your MAIN keyword is the FIRST WORD in your title.

Your store's title is displayed in the top bar of your browser. Here is Dell Computer's title, using 5 most important search words: Dell Laptops, Desktop Computers, Monitors, Printers & PC Accessories.

TIP: Your title should be about 10 words and contain ONLY important words related to your product or service.

Search engines figure that you would only put items in your web site title that are closely related to your website's topic. For example, Dell Computer would not put words in their title talking about "ice cream" when in fact their web site sells computers.

 All versions: Ask your technical pro to put these 10 words in your title for you.

4. Create an "elevator description" of your store

Have you heard of an elevator description? It's when you meet someone getting on an elevator, and you only have until ground floor to tell them exactly what your company does. This will become your **"meta description**."

 TIP: You get up to 25 words for your meta description. Use exactly 25 words if possible!

 TIP: Not every search engine cares about your meta description, because it's so easy to throw in unrelated words. But many do care, and you don't want to ignore them.

5. Have the add-on contribution "All Products" added to your store

Many search engines do not like and cannot see into databases. The "All Products" add-on makes an additional regular web page, the kind that search engines like, listing all of the products in your store.

All versions: Either have your technical pro install this add-on contribution, or use a form of open source commerce that has it pre-installed for you such as CRE Loaded.

6. Now make really juicy web pages that will make search engines sniff all over

Take each of your keywords and make sure you have at least five logical ones on each page. That's what makes the page juicy. Write long product descriptions! Throw a bunch in the welcome on your home page! It's not enough to just let your technical pro hide the search engine codes in your site. You must ALSO have them on your pages for search engines to believe them.

7. Now that you've finished laying all your search engine bait, get listed with FREE Open Directory

If you are accepted by the human editor who reviews your application, you will get picked up by major search engines Google, Netscape Search, AOL Search, Lycos, HotBot, DirectHit, and hundreds of others. Open Directory is the largest, most comprehensive human-edited directory of the Web.

How to get listed with Open Directory:

Give a fact-filled, concise explanation of what your store sells and what your unique angle is in 25-30 words. No hype or sales terms. If you irritate the editor or break their rules, they can choose not to run your listing and your site will not be picked up by most search engines. Listings that are accepted by Open Directory may be picked up by Google and the host of other search engines in a few days to 4 months. You can update your Open Directory listing at any time. www.dmoz.org

8. Make use of free Cross Links

Another thing that makes search engines consider your site more important than others is to have many sites linking to your site and your site to link to other IMPORTANT sites. This is called "cross-linking" when you link to another site and vice-versa.

TIP: "Important" websites are sites that get a LOT of visitors.

All versions: Get the add-on contribution called "LINKS" installed by your technical pro, or use a version of open source commerce that has it pre-installed such as CRE Loaded.

OR simply add a new web page to your website and type links to the other sites (follow instructions in the Jump Start Guide to add a new page). *You will have to add the links to other sites yourself, it will not be automatic.*

The Links add-on allows other sites to *automatically* add links to yours just by filling out a form on your site. (You can set it up so you must approve them first, if you wish.) This is half of the links formula!

Now, the other half of the links formula is to get other sites to list YOUR site on them:

- Search for other open source commerce sites that have "LINKS" installed ("osCommerce AND Links") and fill out the links form on their sites.
- And/or email other sites and request them to add a link to your site.
- Ask any friends who have websites to link to yours.
- Join a "web-ring" of sites of related sites that all link to each other. Find one with a search engine by typing "Web Ring" and your most important keyword.

There are many other things you can do to attract search engines, but these are the ones most relevant to a new open source commerce store. Once you have covered all these basics, ask your technical pro for advanced things you can do.

9. Who should bother with Online Directories?

Most search engine strategists don't place a lot of value on online directories, simply because there is an infinite supply of directories. Anybody can call a web page an online directory and there is nothing to stop them.

The secret is to find online directories that ALSO get a lot of traffic. Like any site that gets a lot of traffic, these are considered "more important" to search engines and will increase your rankings.

If you have a highly-specialized site, for example, wedding supplies, you will do well to sign up with heavily-trafficked online wedding directories.

If you sell to a niche market, I would place 30-day test listings on some of the top-listed directories in your industry, then I would ask my technical pro for a report of "Referral URLs" and see how much of my traffic came from those directories. Divide the cost of the listing by the number of actual sales you received from that link, and you have the total cost per sale.

10. If all else fails, buy your way to the top!

When all else fails, you can buy your way to the top of the page with programs such as Google Ad Words. Your text ad runs for free in the top right column of Google, Earthlink, AOL, and Ask Jeeves. You only pay when someone actually clicks to come to your store. Average cost per click is thirty cents but you choose what to pay.

You do not have to know anything except the keyword information you already filled in above, and how to fill in an online form.

Google Ad Words: http://adwords.google.com/

Yahoo Sponsored Search:

http://searchmarketing.yahoo.com/srch/choose.php

What about ad banners?

If you sell to a niche market, ad banners on "sister websites" may be highly effective and economical. The beauty of the web is that you can reach highly targeted audiences; there is no need to use traditional 'broadcasting" techniques by running an ad on a general-interest site or web portal. "Highly effective and economical" means more than 1% of those who see your ad click it and come to your website, and comes from traditional direct-mail marketing where a 1% response rate is considered excellent.

Don't forget traditional marketing!

Don't think that all marketing for your website has to do with the web. Traditional marketing is as important as ever, and even more so for some businesses. Your use of traditional marketing methods can determine whether your website is an investment that gives you a significant return, or an expense that drags your company down.

QUIZ: Are you using traditional marketing effectively?

To find out whether or not you are using traditional marketing effectively, take this simple test. Give yourself a point for each place you have your website listed:

- Your business cards
- Letterhead
- Invoice forms
- The front door of your store
- Your answering machine recording
- On your product brochures
- On your business vehicle
- Are your product brochures available on your website?
- Do you recommend your website verbally to potential customers who cannot decide now?
- Do your employees recommend it verbally?
- Do you list your web address in the footer or "signature" of each email you send?
- Does your email address match your website?

Twelve points is a perfect score. If you totaled six or less, you are not using traditional marketing effectively. It is time to make your website a working asset!

1. Record a new message referring after-hours callers to your website for information, directions, and store hours.
2. Call your printer and tell them to add your web address to all your forms and make signs for your vehicles.
3. Send your brochure to your technical pro so customers can download them from the Internet in "PDF" format.
4. Have your webmaster create email addresses for you and your employees that match your website.
5. Finally, add it to your email "signature" or the "footer" file that gets attached to every email message you send. To do so in Microsoft Outlook, from the top bar TOOLS, click OPTIONS, then the MAIL

FORMAT tab, the SIGNATURES button, then the NEW button, and follow the directions in the wizard. **TIP**: if you include the www. in your email signature, most recipients can CLICK the link to be taken automatically to your website.

6. Finally, write down your web address and post it on your checkout counter, on your cash register, and in this reminder note to yourself and your employees: HYVOW – *Have You Visited Our Website?*

Incorporate strategic customer feedback

Any time you receive the same feedback from two or more sources, take it very seriously. You may think, "oh that is silly!" but peoples' minds work very differently. Remember that for every piece of feedback you receive, many more thought the same thing but did not bother to tell you.

Ask for more information so you can incorporate the feedback. If they said they did not understand what they were buying, ask them what would have made it clearer. You may suddenly find that a product picture you thought was fine is VERY fuzzy! Or that only half a sentence copied into your product description, and it is missing the other half.

Once you have incorporated the change, you may consider writing to the complainer again and asking them to look at the change. If you can give them a freebie of some sort in exchange for their efforts, or a $5 discount on future purchases, that would be great and they would not feel as if they are doing your work for you. But they are doing something that you cannot. You are the store owner, you look at your store every day, and you have it memorized forwards and back. You cannot see it with the fresh eyes that they can. Your one-time complainer can become one of your greatest allies, advocates, and even friends.

Appendix A:
Sources for finding
technical pros

Chain Reaction Web

http://www.chainreactionweb.com/

Free osCommerce (Zen Cart, CRE Loaded, or osCommerce) installation on hosting account. 50+add-on contribution options included. Real full time support for use or support issues via phone or email 24/7 from the makers of the CRE loaded 6 osCommerce.

Algozone
http://www.algozone.com/

A large selection of themes, layouts and color combinations available for osCommerce and many business types. Support, logo integration and installation services for the templates they sell.

Reece George
http://stores.ebay.com.au/reecegeorge/

Reece George is an Internet marketing professional sourcing 'practical' products for running an online business. His Ebay Australia store sells everything you need for an online business "in a box."

Pithy Productions, Inc.
"We wrote this book!"
http://www.pithyproductions.com/ and
http://www.oscommercemanuals.com/
We cater to technology cowards. Have no fear! We can get you selling on the web. Founded in 1999 by consultant and author of this book Kerry Watson, Pithy Productions Inc. is a full-service firm specializing in turn-key ecommerce installation, customization, and hosting for full-service clients. Flat-rate pricing so there are no surprises. Each new store includes one year of FREE web hosting and FREE unlimited email addresses with your domain name. Contact us today to see if you qualify for a FREE, 100% custom design for your new open source commerce store.

Appendix B:
Pre-Setup Checklist

These questions must be answered to set up your store correctly the first time. It will save you lots of time later if you **take the time now to discuss this with your techie and answer every one. Ask your techie if you do not understand a question; some can seem a little technical.**

NOTE: This can also be found on the web in an easy-to-use form that you can email to yourself or your installer. See Appendix C for the web address for this and many more helpful web-based forms.

Each Item number below corresponds to the number on the next page, the "default" osCommerce setup:

GENERAL	Your Answer:
1. What do you want to be the Page Title that shows in your top browser bar?	
2. What domain name do you want for this store?	
3. What do you want to name your company logo that will be placed in the top left corner in place of the osCommerce logo?	
4. In addition to the top gray navigation bar, do you want an additional navigation bar above the top gray navigation bar? If so, list the link names.	
5. osCommerce includes navigation pictures for My Account, Cart Contents, and Checkout. Do you wish to use these?	

LEFT-COLUMN:	
Do you want to include the following boxes or pages?	
6. Categories	
7. Manufacturers	
8. What's New	
9. Quick Find	
10. Information:	
11. Shipping & Returns	
12. Privacy Notice	
13. Conditions of Use	
14. Contact Us	
15. Custom:	
RIGHT-COLUMN:	
Do you want to include the following boxes or pages?	
16. Bestsellers	
17. Specials	
18. Reviews	
19. Languages	
20. Currencies	
MIDDLE COLUMN:	
21. Do you want to change the heading that reads, "What's New Here?"	
22. What text do you want to be placed below "What's New Here? (approx. 250 words or less)	
23. Do you want to include the box: New Products for (Month)	
PAGE FOOTER:	
24. Do you want a copyright statement for your own company?	
25. Do you want to run affiliate banners in your footer?	
SECTION 2. COLORS & STYLES	
FONTS:	
26. The default font STYLE is Tahoma font. Do you want to change this font style?	
27. The default font SIZE is 12 pixels. Do you	

want to change this font size? (note: substantially changing the size may change all column widths and layouts of your pages)	
28. The default font COLOR for plain text is black. Do you want to change this font color?	
29. The default LINK COLOR is black that changes to gray when you put the mouse over it. Do you want to change these link colors?	
30. The default LINK STYLE is underlined. Do you want to remove the link underlines?	
LOOK AND FEEL:	
31. The default menu bar color is gray. Do you want to change this menu bar color?	
32. The default shape of menu bars is rounded corners. Do you want rounded corners or square?	
OPTIONAL: MY STORE TEXT	
My Store is store settings that will be displayed on different pages throughout the website. You may also do it yourself using the Administrative Module in the Administration-My Store section. If you include it here for your installer, he or she may insert it for you.	
NOTE: The following items are NOT shown on the attached picture.	
33. What is your store name?	
34. Who is the store owner?	
35. What email address do you want customers to email to?	
36. What email address do you want to be displayed as the FROM: address when you send emails to customers?	
37. What country is your store in?	
38. What state is your store in?	
39. Do you want an email notification to be sent to you each time you receive an order?	
40. What is your store's address and phone number?	
41. How many decimal places do you wish to	

show when calculating tax?	
OPTIONAL: PAGE TEXT There are 4 default pages in the Information Box in the LEFT-COLUMN that need your customized text filled in. If you include it here for your installer, he or she can insert it for you. *NOTE: These are NOT shown on the attached picture..*	
42. What do you want to say on the Shipping & Returns page?	
43. What do you want to say on the Conditions of Use page?	
44. What do you want to say on the Contact Us page?	
45. What do you want to say on the Privacy Notice Page?	
SECTION 3. CUSTOMIZATION AND IDENTIFICATION *NOTE: These are NOT shown on the attached picture.*	
46. Do you have a large number of products that need to be entered?	
47. What username and password do you want to use for the Administration screen?	
48. What is your name?	
49. What is your email address?	
50. Do you already own this domain or do you need your installer to get it for you?	
51. Do you want custom matching buttons to match your website's look and feel?	
52. Is there anything else you need to tell your installer about your website?	

Appendix C
List of Cheat Sheets

The following Cheat Sheets are available to our readers on the web at <u>http://www.oscommercemanuals.com/cheatsheets/</u>

PRE-SETUP Checklist for Your Store

52 nitty gritty items that your installer might otherwise have to ask you one at a time. Charts for colors, font sizes and styles. Emails results to you or your installer. Includes **osCommerce-annotated**, a picture of a default osCommerce website numbered to correspond to each item on the checklist, a **<u>Color Selector</u>** so you can see the exact colors you want on the web, and a **<u>font chart</u>** of the most usable web fonts.

InfoBox Checklist

Goes through each and every Information Box on the site from top to bottom and left to right, making sure you are satisfied with the wording and contents of each one. Automatically emails results to you or your installer.

Greetings and Menu Bars Checklists

Goes through every greeting and menu bar to make sure you are satisfied with the wording and contents of each one. Automatically emails results to you or your installer.

Look and Feel Checklist

This guide is built on an actual **style sheet** for osCommerce that has had each style applied to it so you can see exactly what the styles will do. Give to your installer.

Appendix D
Further Resources

Email Groups:

osCommerce for Newbies To join, send a blank email to
osCommerce-Newbies-Subscribe@yahoogroups.com

Choosing an Order Fulfillment Service
http://onlinebusiness.about.com/od/integration/a/fulfillment2.htm

Pick and Ship
http://www.pickandship.com/
Order Fulfillment & Inventory Management
Don't want to become a logistics expert? Want to make the best use of
your time? Want to manage costs? Tired of going to the Post Office?

No matter how small or large your company, logistics can become a cost
center that drains your profitability and limits your growth. Specialty
Fulfillment Center can develop a program to manage your entire
inventory and help you better manage costs and growth.

Fulfillment	**Inventory Management**
Custom pick and pack	Cycle Counts
Web Based order processing	Physical Inventory Counts
Shipping analysis	Activity Reporting
Package analysis	Min/Max level monitoring
Package labeling	SKU control
Insert brochures/flyers	Lot/Batch numbers
Kitting/Light assembly	Pallet storage
National distribution	Break pallet

OH Logistics

http://www.ohlogistics.com/ECommerce_Fulfillment_Services.asp
Call toll-free 877-401-6400 and let us help you deliver on your e-tail
promises. Learn more about how our warehousing solutions can help
your company. Or, if you are ready to request a quote, please choose one
of our convenient methods for submitting a quote request.

Book Masters

http://www.bookmasters.com/
Book fulfillment
Whether it's one book shipped direct to consumer or carton quantities
shipped to trade accounts, BookMasters gives publishers a single source
to manage all their fulfillment and distribution needs.

The Fulfillment House

http://www.thefulfillmenthouse.com/
What makes **The Fulfillment House** different? We handle your
fulfillment and related services YOUR WAY! Want to learn more? Come
inside and see what makes our house, your house!

Jam'n Logistics

http://www.4jlc.com/
Third-party warehousing, distribution and packaging services.
Since1993. For more information on what JLC can do for you please
contact us at info@4jlc.com or call us today, at 323-721-4JLC (4552).

www.ingramcontent.com/pod-product-compliance
Lightning Source LLC
Chambersburg PA
CBHW080426060326
40689CB00019B/4401